DATE DUE

GAYLORD			PRINTED IN U.S.A.

COMPEL

COMPEL

How to Get Others in Your Organization to Think and Act Differently

Robert D. Gilbreath

John Wiley & Sons, Inc.

Library of Congress Cataloging-in-Publication Data:

Gilbreath, Robert D. (Robert Dean)
    Compel : how to get others in your organization to think and act differently /
  Robert D. Gilbreath
       p.   cm.
    Includes bibliographical references.
    ISBN-13: 978-0-470-05145-0 (cloth)
    ISBN-10: 0-470-05145-0 (cloth)
    1. Persuasion (Psychology)—Social aspects.   I. Title.
  HM1196.G55 2007
  303.3'42—dc22

                                                  2006016192

Printed in the United States of America.

10 9 8 7 6 5 4 3 2 1

For Grace, Lily, Ella, and Cecile

Contents

Preface

There were hundreds of them, they had me surrounded, and I was totally alone. Standing above them on the back of a flatbed truck in a gravel parking lot, somewhere way up in the mountains of eastern Kentucky—the deepest holler in Appalachia. Scanning the hundreds of faces I saw disdain, skepticism, and some anger that drizzly Saturday morning. They didn't want to be here and they didn't want to listen to me. But they had to, and so did I. I was sixteen years old and my father put me here.

He was a staff lawyer for the Kentucky Department of Transportation, and this patronage job required him to support an upcoming statewide vote. Seems the politicians in charge wanted to amend the state constitution, and the matter was put before a public referendum. Dad was ordered to go to Harlan County and exhort the state highway employees there to turn out and vote for the amendment. He was shy by nature and detested this assignment. I was on the high school debate team and liked to argue ideas. "I need you to do this for me, son," he said the night before we drove up into the mountains. "You're better at it than me."

So there I stood, looking out at the men and women in overalls, khaki work shirts, and watching them light cigarettes, look at their watches, kick the gravel with steel-toed boots, and spit tobacco juice. Hard-bitten folks who drove dump trucks, laid asphalt, and threw road kill into the back of yellow government pickups for a living. And the kid from the flatlands was going to get them fired up about a constitutional convention to amend laws on usury, eminent domain, and capital gains. Thanks Dad.

That scene occurred almost forty years ago. Between then and now I've done a lot of public speaking. I've addressed graduate students at some of the world's leading business schools, spoken before huge international conferences, and coached executives and government leaders on six continents. I've been on television and radio, created change plans for major corporations—you name it, and I've done this willingly. After all, I'd been to the gravel parking lot.

Getting others to think and act differently seemed magical to me then, a mysterious talent some have and others just don't. But as the years and experience rolled past, I've begun to see patterns—basic steps and common elements in every marketing pitch, popular song, motion picture, and rousing public speech. I've learned that compelling people come in all shapes and have all sorts of talents, but they seem to follow a few basic rules. These rules work and I want to share them with you. I want you to know, believe in, and practice these techniques so you can have an impact, so you can make a dent on people and events in your lives.

Becoming compelling, affecting outcomes through others, is much more than public speaking. It involves crafting dreams, guiding others along them, establishing and enforcing channels of new behavior. It requires a special outlook and a special set of skills, yes—but almost anyone can master them and I've seen many do so. I'll share these stories here.

In all aspects of our personal lives, jobs, and societies, no matter our position or age, we face two risks: (1) Something bad will happen; and (2) Something good will not happen. Those content with exactly the way things are, the defenders of the status quo, worry about the first risk. The compelling among us are obsessed with the second.

I firmly believe that buried inside all of us, no matter our position or capabilities, lies the potential to think and act differently. Those who can energize this latent power, who can bring it to life and use it as an engine of improvement and prosperity—who can compel us, magnetize us to their cause—those are the real leaders in a world that so desperately needs all the good ones it can get.

Introduction

com·pel \ kəm-ˈpel \ *vt* **com·pelled; com·pel·ling**

1. To drive or urge forcefully or irresistibly.
2. To cause to do or occur by overwhelming pressure.

This is a book about power, influence, effectiveness, clout. It's about empowering yourself and your groups to get things done. Using intelligent leverage to make things happen the way you want them to happen. In short, being successful at whatever you choose.

So don't expect to learn how to get along, how to follow the rules, or ways to accept the world around you as you find it. This is about getting others to accept what you're laying down, *making the rules* for others to follow. I'm going to tell you how to harness time-honored, proven mechanisms that work—the keys to getting others to think and act differently. It's not about watching, understanding, or going along with the changes that affect your self, your family, work, and environment, but about making those changes. Affecting the outcomes. Designing and building your world and your future.

In a nutshell, that's the precise definition of *power*— the ability to affect outcomes through others. Think about every successful person you know, every dominant corporation, effective school, military unit, organization, and nation. All share this trait: They acquire and flex as much power as they can and use it to achieve their purpose. Others don't, and that's why we call them unsuccessful. They may be genuine, competent, well-intentioned, and highly motivated. They are often intelligent, educated, well-funded, and even admirable. But when their aims are thwarted, their goals missed, we don't call them leaders and we don't line up to join their cause. Other terms stick—terms like ineffective, incompetent, weak. Or even worse: irrelevant, losers.

The difference between those who win and those who don't can be complex and multidimensional, but it can be reduced to these terms: Winners affect outcomes. Others don't. And like many choices and chances we select over the course of our lives, this one is deceptively simple to understand and hellishly difficult to attain. That's because it hinges on the changes one gets others to accept and embrace. You don't win by keeping things the same. You win by making them different—you win by changing them, by getting others to think and act differently. There are four ways this is done. I call them "change mechanisms." Each one is the subject of a chapter here.

If you understand the essence of power—getting others to achieve the outcomes you desire—and you become proficient at the four change mechanisms, you will gain a tremendous increase in control over your condition, your future, and your life. You'll cease being a mere passenger on the road to the future. You'll be in the driver's seat, your hands on the wheel. You will be a leader.

If this seems blunt or mercenary, it isn't. Power can and does lead to marvelous improvements in all fields. It can elevate people, protect the innocent, advance virtue. Yes, it can be abused, and often is. We'll see that here. We'll learn how the malevolent gain and wield power, using the very mechanisms I prescribe in this book. But knowing these mechanisms and how they can be used against us also serves to increase our power. We become protected from them, skeptical of their hidden allure. Ultimately, we learn that power is *value-neutral*. It can help and hurt. It's like a flaming torch—able to either light up and warm our lives or burn them down. But you simply cannot use "good power" and defend against "bad power" unless you know how it works. Unless you see through all the flags, slogans, dogma, and emblems it's often cloaked in. Peering past these into the heart of power, you will find these four change mechanisms at work, for good or for evil. And you'll be much better off with that knowledge.

❏ A Glimpse into the Gears ❏

When the President of the United States gets on national television at prime time and promotes a new policy or outlines a new national program, he's using a time-honored change mechanism: *Message*. He's in a powerful position to begin with, being the president and all. But he needs to broadcast a new way of thinking and behaving on your part. Whether you stand up and salute or give him an obscene gesture is a function, more often than not, of how he phrases, reinforces, and backs up that message. Nevertheless, agree or not, you get the message.

When your boss initiates a new bonus program, complete with target goals and precise rewards for those who meet them (and often, as well, specific punishments for those who don't), she's engaging the *Reaction* mechanism. She's counting on everyone responding, positively or negatively, to the fears, habits, needs, and values she assumes you all have. How she enforces this, how fair, equitable, and aligned all this is—that's a different story. But the mechanism is there. She is cranking it up to get what *she* wants.

When we get to this one, we'll find that *Reaction* is a troublesome change lever. It can't be counted on nowadays and can often backfire. If you're flogging *Reaction* and not seeing many results, you need to rethink it. You might be wasting your time and energy. You might even be harming your effort.

6

Introduction

When your school grapevine starts buzzing about something, or when chat rooms, blogs, and other networks start vibrating with an idea or opinion, a different change mechanism is at work: *GroupThink*. Others get engaged in the discussion, communities of interest form, take shape, and build. If they reach an effective critical mass or surge beyond a tipping point, stuff happens. Things change. Outcomes, whether emergent from the discussion or deliberately engineered through it, are achieved. This isn't a new phenomenon—we've always had gossip and fickle public opinion. It's just supercharged now, thanks to network technology. Marketers, politicians, and other interest groups are spending billions of dollars to harness this change mechanism. They want you to think and act differently, and this is one of four ways they achieve that outcome.

GroupThink has ancient roots. Think of words like taboo, scorn, peer pressure, and public humiliation when we start describing this one. But don't neglect positive social pressure, like when a hero is celebrated, a celebrity feted, or a sports figure is named "athlete of the week."

Ever wonder why the Red Cross issues "I gave blood" stickers to the donors of your company's blood drive? They're using the *Witnessing* mechanism to get nondonors to give blood. This is especially effective when the ones with the stickers on their shirts or blouses are respected and influential in the company. They're counting on you to mimic them—to follow their lead. Bless their well-intentioned hearts, the Red Cross is then using a power play to shame or otherwise influence you to sign up next time. They're affecting the outcomes they want—more and more freely-given blood for their inventory and sales chain. They know what they're doing.

Yet knowing these mechanisms isn't enough. Knowing *how* to use them, when they're appropriate and when they're not, and being able to skillfully pull them off is the ultimate goal. That's when you've risen to the leadership ranks. I want you to learn them, yes, but I really want you to become satisfied users of them.

❏ Why This Book Is Different ❏

The goal here is simplicity and effectiveness. It's not to impress you or my colleagues, to complicate things so only I can untangle them, or to dress up basic topics in academic gowns. So I'll chose clarity over complexity, the direct over the subtle, and leave the nuances and "well, that depends" to people wanting to impress a professor or pad their resume. That doesn't make me win. I win by getting others (this means you) to think and act differently, too. I win when you learn to win.

Chapter 1

Message

mes·sage \ˈme-sij \ *n*

A usually short communication transmitted by words, signals, or other means from one person, station, or group to another.

Picture this: You're in a bookshop facing a long, rainy weekend. You'd like a book to keep you occupied, interested. The choice boils down to two, and you're having trouble deciding which to buy. Finding a reading chair and table, you open each book to the first sentence on the very first page.

Book #1:
"Mother died today. Or yesterday maybe, I don't know."

Book #2:
"In the summer of 1955, I arranged to join some friends who were going into the Alps."

These are actual first sentences from real books. Which would you choose? They're priced identically, have about the same number of pages, and each is written by a Nobel laureate. I'm going out on a limb here, but my guess is that the overwhelming majority of adults would push Book #2 aside and become absorbed in reading Book #1 on the way to the cash register. Book #1 is *The Stranger* by Albert Camus. Book #2 is *The Double Helix*, by James Watson. Camus won the 1957 Nobel Prize in Literature. Watson, co-discoverer of the structure of DNA, won the 1962 Nobel Prize in Physiology or Medicine. Both books were huge international best sellers.

The opening lines of any book, the introductory notes of any song, and the first few scenes of all movies are "invitations." They invite you to come into the world of the author, performer, or director and spend some time with him. Done correctly, these introductions seize your interest and *compel* you to pay attention. You can learn a lot from them.

Whether you're giving a speech to your company, writing a cover letter for your resume, addressing a child in a moment of stress, or teaching a group of students how to use a software program, you have a golden opportunity to get others to think and act in your way. And these are just examples; hundreds more could be listed. No matter what your job, life role, or dreams, you must learn to invite others into your world or you will be terribly alone. Like Book # 2, you'll be shoved aside.

Here's why. Depending on the situation, you may be competing with a pending divorce, a new car, a video game, a backache, 500 television channels, a house renovation, financial difficulties, an ill child, and/or perhaps plans for a summer holiday. All these items and more crowd the consciousness of all of us, all the time. To penetrate this information fog, this cloud of concern, you need to know a few tricks.

People who write newspapers, produce motion pictures, craft political speeches, design advertising campaigns, and market consumer products have this in common: If their invitation fails, so do they. Our attention spans have only so much shelf space; we can become absorbed in only a few things at any time. Unless your message becomes one of those lucky things, you haven't got a chance in hell of affecting an outcome. You're pushed out of view, turned away and tuned out—dumped back on the shelf. You've missed the first and sometimes last chance to compel, and your competitor—not you—is being taken home.

The invitation is critical, but it's just one of five phases you must master in order to craft and deliver a strong, lasting, and behavior-changing message. We're going to examine the *Message* mechanism in this first chapter because it's vital to becoming compelling. You simply cannot become compelling without it.

❏ Key Principles ❏

This isn't about making you an electrifying TV preacher or riveting stand-up comedienne. Nor is it about inform-

13

ing, instructing, teaching, or entertaining a group. There are other books for that. This is about grabbing others by their attention spans and leaving them so compelled to do what you ask, so driven to follow your lead, that they can't stand doing anything else.

Teaching is good, influencing is better. Compelling is best.

You win when they walk away from your message with a burning desire to act on it. You win when they forget most everything else and avidly pursue the steps you want them to take. The ultimate test of your success with this mechanism is whether they think and act differently than they did before. That's the difference between a compelling message and one that's just interesting, informative, entertaining, or educational.

How many of us have attended seminars, company training sessions, or professorial lectures and walked away with this thought: "That was interesting and quite enjoyable. Now, tell me how this affects my life and what I should do differently?" I've given hundreds of seminars around the world, and I've learned this is my biggest challenge. The worst comment I could hear goes like this: "Real cool, but so what?" You never want to hear that. You want some variation of "Gotta run, gotta start doing what you want me to do!"

Message

When you're in a position to establish a message among others, don't fear that they will not like you, won't understand you, or won't agree with you. Those are minor irritants. The real fear, the one that should guide you in every aspect of communicating to compel, is that they will consider you *irrelevant*.

Message Explained

A good message should be a common one. Everyone should get it and understand it in the same way. It must be clear, memorable, and actionable. Other change mechanisms we'll describe follow the message. They reinforce it, strengthen it, guide people in implementing it. The goal is urgency, a far-reaching, undeniable effect on everyone involved. You want your message to be in the forefront of their consciousness, and you want the instructions it contains to dictate what they think and what they do.

It's easy to imagine a corporate, community, or family leader delivering such a message, but they're not the only ones who do. You do, all of us do. It can be compelling if it follows this design:

- First, the "Invitation." This is the critical beginning— your narrow window of opportunity, your only chance to seize the attention and direct the desires of others.
- The second step is called "Empathy." Here's where you earn the right to command attention and dictate the rules of thought and behavior you want.

- The third step is called "Development." This is the logical structure of your argument or proposition, the meat and potatoes of your message. Done correctly, development converts your target group from interested observers to enlisted supporters.
- The fourth step in this progression is termed the "Dream." This is where you envision a world where your message is acted upon. You paint a picture of the future you desire and place each individual within it. You guide them into imagining what could be if only they think and act differently—along the lines you've laid out.
- Finally, and oh, so importantly, comes the fifth step, "Challenge." Here you make clear exactly what each person or affected group must do to achieve the Dream. You give them their marching orders, telling them what they should do first thing Monday morning.

I know, I've set out to explain four change mechanisms, and here I'm breaking the very first one into a further five steps. Don't worry about this. The steps follow naturally, one after the other, and you're going to recognize them quickly. That's because so many successful songs, books, speeches, and movies are purposefully designed this way. This isn't coincidence. It's because these steps work, and compelling people know they work.

Table 1.1 is a quick look at the five steps to a mes-

Table 1.1   Anatomy of all Messages

Element	Question Answered	Goal
1 Invitation **2** Empathy	Why should I listen?	I can't put this down, can't tune it out. This is for me.
3 Development **4** Dream	Why should I care?	I share this belief and concern. I know this is true and I want it.
5 Challenge	What should I do?	I am passionate about this and will change accordingly.

sage. Every compelling message, regardless of medium or subject, contains these five elements, in this order, to achieve these objectives.

Let's look at each of these, see if they make sense, see their power.

Step #1: INVITATION—Seizing their Attention Spans. Know this: No matter your audience—one person or an entire nation, the scarcest resource here is not money, time, or knowledge. It's their attention span. It's crowded, full of competing thoughts and concerns, and it has the half-life of a subatomic particle. You must seize it and stretch it out for as long as it takes to achieve your goal. There are a few ways to do this.

Entice: Lure them into your story. Open with a question, a dilemma, something—anything—that makes them stop and listen. Your enemy here is apathy, best described as the "Who cares?" reaction. Not dog bites man, but man bites dog. Not "Today we will be discussing the financial results of last quarter," but "We're winning and I'm going to tell you why!" Not "A history of the etiology of global warming and a review of geophysical implications," but "We're going to boil to death."

> **The Invitation should take 2 to 3 sentences, maximum. It should be delivered slowly and seriously.**

Confuse: Start with a statement or story that doesn't make sense, something that seems counterintuitive, off-base. Something that goes against conventional wisdom. The audience will want an explanation. They'll want to hear you out. They'll let their minds stick around to see where this goes. Mission accomplished. Your invitation works. Naturally, you'll need to unravel the confusion your way—you'll have to start making sense pretty quickly. That's up to the next few steps. But you won't get to them without a carefully designed invitation.

Dare: You picture a new world and challenge or shame them into running after it. You dream big, make audacious claims, issue dares. Don't be ludicrous here — challenges must be attainable. But they must also be *compelling*. I know of no factory worker who jumps out of bed Monday morning and, as soon as her feet hit the floor, starts dreaming "I just can't wait to go to the plant today and raise the return on shareholder investment to 9 percent!" Challenges must be presented in terms that evoke response — no one chases an abstraction. Challenges must be personal — something the receiver can identify with.

Promise: Here you hold out a proposition, a deal. "Work with me on this, and you will be rewarded." This is the most popular invitation I've seen, but it's also the most dangerous. You can get in big trouble if you over- or under-promise. And if you can't come through with the prize, you will really be devalued. Be careful with your promises, with the advantages you cite. If you can't guarantee them, don't make them. The problem with promises is that if they're easy to attain, they don't hold much persuasive value. And if they're difficult to attain, you face a big risk of failure to come through. Of the four invitation techniques I've described, *Promise* would be my last choice.

Suppose you're in a meeting of the organizers of a charity foundation. Ask a question like this: "Would any of you want to know how we can triple charitable donations while serving ten times as many people as we do now?" (Enticement) The CFO of a major corporation (these guys are not known for presentation style) may begin by saying "We're doing so much business, we're selling ourselves into bankruptcy." (Confusion) A football coach might start off like this: "I'm looking at all you guys here and notice not a one of you is wearing a championship ring. I wonder if you ever will." (Dare) And mom and dad might sit down with junior and say "We've been thinking about you. We believe there is a way for you to have a new car by Christmas." (Promise) Those of you with teenaged children now know why I say the *promise* technique is the least advisable.

Finally, don't stretch the invitation out any longer than absolutely required. If your message is a newspaper, say, think of this as the headline, not the entire story. Quick, sharp, powerful, and inviting—that's the goal.

Before we get into step two, let's revisit the two books we began with. Turn back to the opening of this chapter and look the first sentences over for a moment. Book #1, *The Stranger*, leaves the reader with a host of concerns and questions: Why doesn't he (or she) know? Where is he, where is his mother? Doesn't he care about his mother? How did she die? Was there foul play? Is he her murderer? Is he a child, adult? What gives? This is a great invitation, and Camus is a master at grabbing your attention from the get-go.

As for Watson, let's just say he'd better stick to his day

job of unwinding nature's deepest scientific mysteries. Sure, the book did very well, but no thanks to this opening. It sold because he was world famous and everyone already had an interest in the topic. Had you not known of him or his achievement, after reading the first sentence you probably would expect a snoozing recitation of his vacation trip, complete with slides. It's easy to tell which of these two guys won the Nobel for Literature.

Look around, and you will find carefully designed and engineered invitations everywhere. Disney World knows this. While you're waiting in sweltering weather to enter a particular attraction, they've planned "invitation" spaces for you. There is some bit of entertainment to draw you in, some minor amusement that conditions you in what to expect. A bit of enticement to help you get ready for the great experience to come. Books use a preface for the same reason—inviting, conditioning, ramping in. Real estate developers always build "welcoming space" into new subdivisions. This is their entrance gate, the landscape that draws you into the place. It serves two purposes: It softens the entry blow from a freeway into a residential enclave, and it sets the stage for your experience of the quiet, safe, refined world they want you to join. It ramps you down from the frenetic world of traffic and commerce and, most importantly, into their world. You're irresistibly drawn in. That's compelling.

Okay, you've given a good invitation and you've got their attention. Now what?

Step #2: EMPATHY—You Are Like Them, but Unlike Them. Almost every U.S. President in my lifetime has opened a televised speech with some version of these words: "My fellow Americans. . . ." Three simple words, but Democrats and Republicans alike, over many decades, have chosen to begin their remarks this way. Why? They just as easily could say "Hey everybody, listen up . . ." or "I would like to present next year's fiscal budget," or even "Last spring the first lady and I had a wonderful vacation in the Alps." But no, they use those other three words to establish *Empathy*—the delicate balance of power between them and us. They need to be like us and unlike us at the same time. This isn't easy to do. After all, they're presidents! They're most certainly not very much like us. But yet "My fellow Americans" says they *are*. They're citizens of the same nation, they carry the same values, they're sitting in our seats, walking a mile in our shoes. In short, because of this split identity (like us and unlike us at the same time), because of both their distinctiveness and their sameness, they've earned the right to demand our attention and prescribe our future. Pretty compelling. Now, let's find out how you can do this magic act and why it's so important.

Empathy earns you the right to enter into their minds.

I chose the term *Empathy* because that's exactly what you need to establish to be compelling. The dictionary defines it as "Identification with and understanding of another's situation, feelings, and motives." Big point here: Unless you can establish empathy, you're likely to be viewed as interesting but not relevant, nice but not necessary—a person with an opinion. But don't we all have opinions? What's so special about you? "So what?" they'll ask. "What do you know about me, about my job, family, hobby, or life? Who are you to tell me anything?" Expect this objection any time you start to communicate. It doesn't matter if you're standing before an audience, on the phone in a conference call, introducing yourself to a prospective client, or counseling a patient.

You need to show some battle scars, earn the right to enter their consciousness. Otherwise you're from Mars— you just got here. What do you know? Who are you to teach me anything? Unless you're the President, you've got to establish relevancy quickly. The Empathy step is where you move from having their attention to having their respect.

Suppose you're a homeowner attending a zoning board meeting. You get the microphone to express your concerns about a new development in your neighborhood. Don't start by saying "This thing sucks and I want no part of it." That may indeed be how you feel, but just having the microphone doesn't mean you have anyone's respect. Better to begin by establishing your credentials—your right to have a say in the matter. Better to say "I've lived in Eastside for forty years. My kids all graduated from Eastside High School. Now, I think . . . ." Wow, this lady is invested in our community. She's one of us! She has the right to have an opinion on this question.

Compelling people must establish empathy—they must demonstrate they have paid their dues and earned the privilege of expressing their views. These dues don't have to be high—just a little empathy with and understanding of your audience. Ignore deferring to them at your peril. Every culture in history has rejected an invasion of the "other," that is, unless the "other" has something in common with the insiders. Show that commonality.

Now, to the part about being *unlike* them, being *uncommon*. This suggestion seems counter to what I've just written. How can you earn their empathy by showing some commonality with them and yet stand apart—be different?

You do this by isolating one credential, one characteristic that sets you apart from the crowd. If you were identical to your audience you'd have nothing to offer that they don't already have. No news they don't already know—nothing they couldn't get on their own. Surely there is some special perspective, some unique twist on things you can leverage here.

Consider reporters on the network TV news shows.

All of them want to spend a little time in a war zone, despite its being dangerous and uncomfortable. They think that this gives them distinction. When they return to the desk, they can speak with authority—they are literally bringing us "reports from the front." A politician knows that it's shrewd, when appearing on a Sunday morning talk show, to mention that he or she just returned from a visit to the war zone, the devastation of the hurricane, or the site of a drought. This makes them special, in-the-know. Why else would we listen to them?

The point is to find this distinction and use it. It doesn't have to be major, but it should be a real distinction. All people want to hear from experts, authorities, or just folks who have seen something—experienced something—they haven't. Gaining their empathy has this element: I am like you, yet in this regard, I'm special. Therefore, it will be worth your while to hear me out.

With this hard-won position in the minds of your audience, the last thing you want is to blow your message now. So far it's been a battle to gain their attention and respect. Now you must lay out your message logically and simply. It's time to understand the next step: *Development*.

Step #3: DEVELOPMENT—The Heart of Your Message. We like to think our world is logical, that reasonable people can discriminate between logical arguments and fallacious ones—that despite tragedies and accidents, logic rules. If we're concerned about energy conservation, safety, and health, we should logically favor sports and entertainment that promote these goals. If so, then how does one explain NASCAR?

Here's a sport that glorifies speed, danger, and risky driving. Teams and sponsors create the most fuel-gobbling vehicles on earth and race them around ovals, for no utilitarian purpose whatsoever, at reckless abandon. Each car is plastered with sponsor decals that promote, what? Dental hygiene, safe sex, literacy, exercise, proper diet? Not on your life. Instead, the screaming machines roar through exhaust clouds of carbon dioxide and billowing tire smoke in the Winston Cup (cigarettes), or the Busch (beer) series. They proudly exult the benefits of Miller beer, Snickers candy bars, and Viagra. These are hardly staples of life.

And they all drive cars that bear no resemblance to the ones we own. The vast majority of Americans drive SUV's, minivans, pickup trucks, and imports. None of these are on the track. They're all Ford, Chevrolet, and Dodge sedans.

Let's see how this works: These cars are unlike ours, they promote unhealthy and dangerous products, waste energy, pollute the atmosphere, and encourage aggression on our highways. Yet NASCAR is America's fastest-growing "sport"! Main message: Logic doesn't rule.

Other forces and factors are driving individuals and groups—not just at the race track, but everywhere. People throng to NASCAR events seeking excitement, thrills, adventure, an escape from the mundane and mandatory elements of their lives. All of these trump logic, all the time.

Such factors are much more pervasive and powerful than logic alone—factors like hope, excitement, fear, greed, pride, you name it. Comparing logic to these titans of emotion is like comparing a pocket knife to a chainsaw.

Not only does logic pale in comparison, *it often doesn't even make sense*. It simply doesn't work on its own. Logic, as we know it, can be misleading, erroneous, and just plain stupid. So there are two challenges here: (1) People aren't logical; and (2) Logic isn't logical. You need to know why.

We'll struggle to make sense of this dilemma during our discussion of the development stage. We'll use logic, but never depend on it to carry our message into the hearts and minds of living human beings—real people who do, in fact, hope, fear, dream, hate, love, envy, resent, and cherish.

Building your Development Element

The development phase is one I can outline, make into a process. I can point out its four elements very readily. How you flesh them out is up to you, but you must address them in this exact sequence:

Analysis→Diagnosis→Prescription→Prognosis

This sounds like what happens when you visit the doctor, and that's no coincidence. Medical professionals can pretty much skip the first two phases—they don't need to get your attention (you're half nude in their examining room) and they don't need to establish their credentials or earn empathy (they are licensed doctors; you are paying for their advice). So they jump over *Invitation* and *Empathy* and get right to the *Development* phase.

> **Structure your development with clear (not necessarily logical) progressions. Load it with living facts and memorable statistics.**

Anyway, in plain language, this sequence (analysis through prognosis) is actually:

What's wrong that must be righted→

  →What will happen if action isn't taken→

    →What each individual should do about it→

    →What you can expect if you do it.

> **Every new thought goes on trial for its life in this game, and the prosecution (doubt) gets its evidence in first. You're counsel for the defense.**

Message

Suppose you were seated in a conference room and a respected speaker, an expert in her field, earned your attention (invitation) and regard (empathy), but then proclaimed the amazing discovery that 2+2=5? Her argument and her very esteem would crumble immediately. On the other hand, if she proclaimed that 2+2=4, you'd immediately catch up on some snooze time—logical, but so what? You must be logical, but that's not enough; you must be *compelling*—and the two are not the same. Being logical lets you into the arena. Being compelling lets you win there.

Weak and Strong Facts

I was at a cocktail reception after giving a speech to a group of Gallup executives (the respected worldwide polling company) and their clients. The scene was the Plaza Hotel in New York and I was chatting with Cal Martin, the Chief Operating Officer of Gallup. I vividly recall one comment he made: Of all the indicators Gallup has found to predict happiness and high morale among a corporation's employees—the result of thousands of surveys and interviews made under the most scientific conditions—the one question that determined whether morale was sky high or in the toilet was this: "Do you have a good friend at work?"

Of all the factors, cofactors, correlations, weighted averages, and "statistically significant" findings their Ph.D.s in statistics could gin up, this one was the top.

Nothing about your pay, working conditions, vacation allotment, benefits, boss, or prestige. Nope, just if you have a good friend at work.

I remember this because it was simple and direct, but most importantly, because it was *human*. It dealt with something I could hold onto—a simple thing, really: friendship. A companion, someone to share the joy and pain of the workaday world. Someone in whom to confide, complain, someone to celebrate with. A friend at work. Simple, powerful, revealing—and very compelling.

Facts are weak forces when they have no human foundation. Gallup could have rolled out bar charts, scatter diagrams, statistical analyses, the whole scientific basis for their data set; I would have forgotten it all. If you want to build a compelling logical argument you should learn from this story. Load your facts and logic with real, live, human interpretations. Put them into terms everyone can relate to. Humanize the numbers.

Numbers without a human touch mean nothing.

For example, most of us have been taught that the age of the earth is estimated to be around 4 billion years. That's 4,000,000,000. Sounds big, but doesn't mean much. Four billion is just a huge number, a lot, a whole lot. But I can't relate to it. Once you go past a couple of million years, it all seems to blend together into something beyond my comprehension, much less my experience. Now consider this explanation instead:

We all have read of eccentrics who let their fingernails grow to outlandish lengths. Takes them years and years, and some fingernails have grown as long as 48 inches! Imagine how long it takes for a fingernail to grow to that length. Now know this: If your fingernails were growing for as long as the earth has been here, they would circle the earth at the equator four times!

I once watched a noted scientist trying to explain the notion of a nanosecond. A nanosecond is one billionth of a second. I get lost imagining this. The shortest interval I can humanly comprehend is a tenth of a second, or maybe, at a stretch, one-hundredth of a second. I marvel at the fact that a sprinter can set a world record by edging out another guy by one one-hundredth of a second! Wow! But one billionth of a second?

Then the scientist did something quite remarkable. She reminded us that the speed of light was around 186,000 miles per second. We all know we can talk on the phone across continents and it seems like we are in the presence of the person at the other end of the line. Light and electricity travel that fast. She held up a length of copper wire one foot long. "This," she pronounced, "is how far light travels in one nanosecond." A collective gasp arose from the crowd. This woman was a master at humanizing numbers.

Facts lend themselves to comparisons, and comparisons are very compelling. Long after you've heard that Americans spend so many billions on gambling each year, you'll remember that we spend more money on gambling than we do on books, music, and movies combined. That's a fact that sticks. Here's another powerful impression: We spend more, as a nation, on pet food than we do on disabled veterans.

See where I'm headed? Facts and statistics are cold abstractions. Humans are warm beings, not information-processing machines. And if you truly want to get others to think and act differently, your job is not to be factual but to be compelling.

An important tip for creating a compelling Development phase is to avoid mixing the minor and major elements of your argument. If your proposal has five benefits, four huge and one trivial, drop the fifth one. Build your development up, saving the best for last. Don't weaken the benefits by including the little stuff, no matter how good it is. It detracts from your power.

Incidentally, I used the Gallup data soon after I learned of it. I was working in South Africa for a group of gold and diamond mine owners. They were struggling to integrate black miners into supervisory ranks at their various operations. It wasn't working very well. I suggested they promote deserving black candidates in pairs, two at a time, to work in their new roles together. Rather than being isolated and alone in these positions, they now had "a good friend at work." The program was a big success. All those Ph.D.s and scientists at Gallup were onto something. But I never would have known it or done anything about it unless it had been put into human terms.

Human Perception is Biased

Some say this fact is sad, the reason for so many of humankind's mistakes: We're uninformed, confused, we rely on instincts just a bit above animal level. Others praise this lapse, seeing in it the very essence of humanity—people aren't computer programs. We have free will, souls, and hearts. If you want to be compelling, these last aspects of humanity are your allies.

The people on the other end of your message *are* humans, they aren't logical, and—here's the surprise—*they don't need to be*. Logic as we know it was first envisioned by ancient Greek philosophers, the most famous of these being Aristotle. He struggled against "the brute in us" by creating a durable system of logic to guide all our decisions. And for more than two thousand years, all those geniuses in Cambridge, Oxford, the Sorbonne, and Harvard read his works and fashioned world views around them. Give him all the credit in the world, he was *almost* right. But the brute in us still exists, and it guides our decisions much more effectively than logic does. This is important to you, because your goal is to shape people's decisions your way. If you rely on logic alone, you might very likely become an articulate, sophisticated irrelevancy; you could become a professor in a cob-webbed basement of an ancient institution watching the illogical among us rule the world outside.

Knowing how the world works is nice. Knowing how to make the world work your way is better.

Remember, to become compelling, your first job is to reach others where they live, in ways they hold dear. You don't need to teach them or straighten them out. That's the job of ministers, philosophers, mathematicians, and utopians. I give these all the support they need, and wish them well. But just by being logical, they aren't making the world work their way. Unless they affect outcomes (the goal of becoming compelling), we don't even remember their names, much less their arguments.

Our Lives Are Illogical

Consider the most life-altering decisions each of us makes—decisions like which religion to follow, which person to marry, where to work, what fields to pursue, and whether to have children or not. I can't imagine more profound challenges or more difficult decisions. These are the milestones in our lives, the signposts of who we are, what we've done, what we leave behind when we depart. Do we use logic in determining these?

No, no, and no. Statistics prove that most people are of a particular religion because that's the one their parents held. They're born into it, had no choice, didn't rationally consider alternatives. They were raised to believe in a set of precepts, saw that modeled by their parents, witnessed it in churches and schools selected by their parents, and surprise—they adopted it. Yet, our parents became our parents by chance and luck—no one chose them. For most humans, chance and luck dictate religious belief.

Chances are you met your spouse with the same degree of coincidence. In a bar, at a school function, on a vacation, at work. That accounts for about 95% of prenuptial encounters. How many of us went on a worldwide talent search, interviewed thousands of candidates, evaluated each according to a fixed set of criteria, and chose matrimony to the ultimate "weighted-best average" individual? No logic here either, just chance and luck.

> **If logic ruled the world, all our presidents and prime ministers would be math professors!**

Where you currently work is more likely the result of whom you know in your limited sphere of friends, relations, and acquaintances, a chance encounter with a recruiter, an ad on an Internet job board at the right time, or the ephemeral needs of a few hiring companies in your home town. Chance and luck again.

There is no logic in the world that dictates having children. They are expensive, time-consuming, often thankless, and the source of various petty or serious complications and anguish over many, many years. Yet we continue to have them, even when technology and changes in moral values provide us with the "no thanks" option. Begetting kids is human, yes (thank God)—but not logical.

Being Illogical Is Not Being Stupid; It's Being Human

Every second of every waking hour we are bombarded with perceptual stimuli. Our senses are mobbed with competing inputs, so many that no human can possibly pay attention to even a fraction of them. To keep from being overwhelmed, from being driven crazy by this onslaught, we've got to find ways to separate the important from the unimportant—the meaningful from the trivial or inconsequential. We need some sort of filters or automatic judging mechanisms that we can rely on without thinking, some mental rules that sort all this out for us, and that bother our minds with only those things that have some bearing on our survival and advancement. These must be unconscious rules, for no one can possibly consider each impression and decide whether to pay attention to it or ignore it. There are just too many, coming too rapidly. How do we cope?

Message

The answer isn't to be considerate, thoughtful, or even logical in choosing what to attend to and what to discard. The answer is to use bias—built-in preferences for, or reversion to, certain types of input. Perceptual biases help us make sense out of a chaotic assault of information, the unrelenting attack of data, impressions, and images we face at all times. These biases aren't voluntarily chosen. They're the result of millions of years of evolution—of trial and error, successes and mistakes, that brought us here and shaped the way we view the world and how we think about it.

Historians, paleontologists, and anthropologists often differ when putting time frames around the human experience. They argue over which versions of hominids led to our current Homo sapiens species and which were dead ends. They estimate very different time spans regarding how long we've actually been here, in our present form and capacity. But given conservative estimates based on evidence available, let's assume today's human beings have been around for about one million years. Now consider that civilization, even with the widest definition, has been around, at most, 25,000 years. That's the earliest time at which people began to live in settlements, farm and herd animals, write, or divide labor. With these conservative time frames in mind, we see that civilized humans have been on this earth for 25,000 years, while our prehistoric ancestors dwelled here for 975,000 years, or 40 times as long. The uncivilized age of our race is 40 times that of the civilized period. Primitive, uncivilized life had 40 times as long to develop than civilized versions. It stands to reason that human beings, and our perceptual biases, were shaped then—and not in the relatively recent 25,000 years.

So let's look at what forces and factors operated then. Let's do so because primitive conditions are 40 times as important, as powerful, and as lasting as the last 25,000 years.

We've been simple a whole lot longer than we've been sophisticated.

Evolutionary theory tells us that, over time, traits that favor survival and reproduction dominate over those that don't. For animals, these traits are physical: type of fur, length of legs, strength of teeth, swiftness of gait. Humans aren't exempt from these physical restraints and advantages, but we are different from the rest of earth's animals. We have experienced *cultural* evolution. Cultural evolution selects those that will survive and reproduce as efficiently as does physical evolution. Groups that banded together into mutually-supporting tribes fared better than solitary hunters or gatherers. Groups that protected children prevailed in the evolutionary race over those that ignored them. And those that developed language had the advantage over those that just grunted, shrieked, or pointed their fingers at the world.

We are the current result of both physical and cultural evolution, and our perceptive biases demonstrate this profoundly. For 97.5 percent of our evolutionary history, primitive forces and needs shaped us. For the last 2.5 percent, first weak, then stronger civilized factors came into play. Needless to say, primitive forces and needs created almost all of what we are and how we behave. These provide the key to understanding our perceptual biases and, most importantly, how we can use, misuse or overcome them.

Our Uneven Mirrors

We need to understand and use *illogic* to compel others. We are not programmed machines. We are illogical, and our perceptions are biased. The father of all deductive reasoning—the set of principles that rule all rational inquiry in our time—is Francis Bacon, an Englishman who lived from 1561 to 1626. Bacon wrote, "The human mind resembles those uneven mirrors which impart their own properties to different objects . . . and distort and disfigure them."[1] This from the man who *invented* the scientific method—the clear, rational way to examine things without bias. Even this champion of logic and experiment conceded that humans are illogical. It's time to take a look into these "uneven mirrors." Let's start with the biggest biases.

The Simple over the Complex

Compared to contemporary living, our past was very simple. We were driven to fill basic needs: food, shelter, clothing, sex. We ran from or fought simple threats: predatory animals, stormy weather, rival tribes. And when we looked out on our world we saw it in these terms: What can help us or hurt us? We saw the sun and moon, vegetation, streams and rivers, our dwellings, and we saw each other. Pretty simple, basic stuff. Direct, tangible, and fairly predictable objects and events ruled our lives. As Will Durant writes, "All psychology, philosophy, statesmanship, and utopias must make their peace with these biological laws."[2] No anthropologists cite examples of a prehistoric fascination with budget deficits, quantum theory, chemistry, or epistemology. These came later, once the simple tasks and direct threats had been understood and mastered—when the conquering of basic needs yielded enough time and comfort to ponder the complex questions we seem so involved with today.

Living in a subsistence and survival mode was, and remains, in Thomas Hobbe's words "nasty, brutish and short."[3] It is also very straightforward. Should there arise a ponderer, a person or group infatuated with underlying meanings, indeterminate effects, or ultimate universal forces, he would most likely have been caught off guard, unprepared, or eaten alive while the more direct and unconfused lived to reproduce more of their kind. We've had hundreds of thousands of years to hone this preference, this bias in what concerns us. Only recently, relatively speaking, have we been able to consider and wrestle with complexities. That's why *simple* trumps *complex* in gaining our attention and mobilizing our resources. Among the universal archetypes of human thinking, simplicity is a keystone preference.

The simple can be understood readily and dealt with expeditiously. We can figure it out and act on it quickly. Most of us can master it, live through it. Complexity is another story. Understanding complex relationships or phenomena takes talent, time, and training. These are all luxuries confined to the very recent epoch, and to the very select few among us even today. These relationships among forces, factors, and theories are sometimes indirect and often undependable. You simply cannot count on finding foolproof answers or being able to employ them to better your living conditions. Understanding complexity is a gamble reserved for the secure and satisfied, and even among these relatively few, it takes effort and skill. That's why so few of us, even in our multifaceted world, pursue the difficult questions or quest after vague, indeterminate answers. For the vast majority of humans, simple is best. Simple is actionable and direct. Simple works.

No wonder people look for simple explanations to baffling problems. No wonder leaders take intricate issues and boil them down to basic choices. We don't prefer to view other nations as multidimensional, diverse, robust, and intricate. We want them to be cast as friends or foes, allies or enemies. We want simple characterizations and basic distinctions. Leaders know that to mobilize an army of young men and women to risk their lives for a subtlety or suffer hardship for a nuance is virtually impossible. No recruit is driven by the need to reshuffle the balance of trade among geopolitical forces, to break the hegemony of a regional power broker, or to expand a sphere of economic influence. Better to enlist in a fight to protect your homeland and way of life. Better to defeat the infidels, the subhumans, the monsters at our door. Keep it simple when you want to goad others into action. And the more preposterous, or counterintuitive that desired action may be, the simpler and more direct your cause must be.

In order to get others to do something, leaders, corporate managers, priests, city councilmen, and others in positions of authority de-complexify issues and events. They make nuance vanish and they blunt distinctions. Things then become black and white, yes or no, friend or foe. That makes them readily understood and easily actionable. People, on the whole, can then understand what is "out there" and what they must do about it. Intricate or elaborate issues may engage a minority of solitary thinkers, but they never send the masses to the barricades. The lesson in this for the powerful, or would-be powerful, is also simple: If you can't reduce your cause to a simple bipolar crusade, you can't get people to follow you in it. This can work, but it has a very dark side.

> **Simplifying things can be a force for good and evil. To become compelling, you must learn both sides of the blade.**

The Dark Side of Simplification

A prime example is the stereotyping of entire groups of diverse individuals as one monolithic emblem—one simple "thing." This is how a complex society with deep cultural roots and a diversity of views and talents suddenly becomes "the Huns," as the Germans were depicted by the allies in World War I; "the Gooks," as the Vietnamese people became to many American soldiers in the Vietnam War; or "fags," as homosexuals are labeled by those who somehow oppose them (not to mention the terms and attitudes many whites had—and have—for people of color).

It works in the other direction as well; difficult-to-understand principles become dogma because they are styled as good, virtuous, or ideal. The Holy Trinity of many Christian beliefs—that one God may have three separate yet indivisible godheads (God the Father, Christ, and the Holy Spirit) is impossible to accept or defend on grounds of logic alone. Great theologians and philosophers ranging from St. Augustine to Neitzche couldn't put forth a compelling argument for this condition. But—make belief in this conundrum mandatory for the faithful, and condemn those who don't accept it as heretics, and suddenly an imponderable becomes an axiom—an untested and accepted belief. The many questions of: "Why is this?," "How can this be?," "What does this mean?," and "How does this square with observation?" become moot. The question reverts to belief or non-belief. Grace or Sin. Us or Them. Good or Bad. That's the power of simplification—tapping into our primeval roots to harness this built-in bias for the simple over the complex—for the direct over the indirect, tangible over intangible, pronounced over subtle, labels over understanding.

You'll see this everywhere you look, and hear it every time you listen today. Television commercials take a multidimensional human and turn him or her into good or bad solely because they use or don't use a particular deodorant. People who purchase one brand of automobile are wise; those who choose another are dumb. Students who attend a neighboring university are bad; those who attend ours are good. The Germans are industrious, the British effete, the Japanese diligent, the Italians indolent, the Americans spoiled. People who don't follow our religious tenants are destined to hell. Those who do are guaranteed a place in heaven. Pretty simple.

Simplifying others (seeing whole groups as good or bad, advanced or primitive, chosen or not chosen) commonly leads to intolerance of them. Look at any hate group and you'll be able to sum up their message on a bumper sticker—hate thrives on simplicity. Primitive thinking is not a relic of the past; it is with us in many guises today. Enlightened individuals break free from these constraints and resist these simplifying influences through broad exposure to other peoples, ideas, and ways of living. They explore outside their comfort zones, travel, read, and consider alternatives beyond those immediately apparent or readily accessible. This is how they become educated and how they develop wisdom. This is also why, in most cases, the most educated and wise among us are the most tolerant of others, the most open to debate, and the most curious about complex topics. They know that the simple life is indeed "nasty, brutish, and short" and have chosen to rise above it.

Forced simplification naturally leads to the "dumbing down" of ideas and attitudes. To resist this flattening of dimensions into one or two requires vigilance, bolstered by broad education and exposure to varying beliefs, thoughts, lifestyles, and cultures. The more you see and understand the multi-faceted aspects of any subject, be it a people, religion, or scientific theory, the more you are able to escape the fallacies of simplification and the errors they bring.

We are naturally biased towards the simple. But that doesn't mean we should be ruled by it. Be very careful when tempted to oversimplify your *Message*. Unless you're dealing with very primitive folks, you could be headed for disaster.

Now to the next most important bias.

The Current over the Past/Future

Most cultures divide time into three stages: the past, present, and future. Two of these three are complex, indeterminate, and hazy. These are the past and the future. Only one is fairly straightforward, able to be examined, and fairly indisputable—the present, the now. The present is simpler than the past or the future. This is one reason for our next bias: We are much more concerned about the present than either the past or the future. When given a choice among them, we zero in on the present. That's where we "are," where we can do things, make a difference. In our quest to maximize our life experiences, most of us consider the past as irrelevant and the future as unknown. Better to seize the day. Better to deal with what *is*, rather than what *was* or *will be*.

"Now" is one of the most compelling words in our vocabulary.

We see the present as something we can deal with, something we can affect. The past can't be changed and the future can't be foreseen, so why bother with them?

This is a fairly universal bias and need not be examined in great detail. It just makes sense to be more interested in ongoing struggles and activities than those that are over or those that are yet to arrive. No one can change the past, and few can change the future—and even those who can don't know to what extent or why. So we live, work, and think in the *now*. Rather than dive into metaphysics here, let's simply understand what this means for us.

First, it means that urgency and immediacy have precedence over everything else in our lives. Want to get others to help you? Appeal to a present threat, an immediate opportunity rather than some possibility off into the future. Want to build a compelling story? Talk or write about what's affecting us now. If you run the government health agency, don't talk about the black plague of the medieval period or even the influenza pandemic of 1918–21. Talk of bird flu and SARS and West Nile and AIDS if you want funding for epidemiology initiatives. Write editorials about the current threat, the present danger. Invoke immediacy—the situation is getting out of hand. Forget about what it might lead to a century hence—that doesn't get anyone moving.

A Glance at Other Common Biases

The preference we all have for the simple and the immediate are our two most telling biases. But we have many others, all bred into us over millennia. Let's quickly review what we prefer over what we don't. Use this list to judge how compelling your *Message* is.

- **The powerful over the weak.** We pay attention to whatever can impact us in a big way, and not what might have a light effect on our safety or well being. We pay homage to strong leaders, not weak ones. We believe in strong myths and respect strong institutions. We may sympathize with the weak, be it a person or an idea, but we're compelled by strength.
- **The direct over the subtle.** This is a variation on the previous bias, but a distinctive one nonetheless. Direct threats are more insistent than indirect ones. Direct people, for better or worse, gain our attention more readily than refined ones. And subtle messages with faint nuances lose to blatant, undeniable ones in the battle for our attention.
- **The necessary over the optional.** Make your goals necessities, not just "nice to have."
- **The predictable over the possible.** It's wiser to prepare for what *will be* than what *might be*. You can't stay ready for everything, but you can for a few known things.
- **The absolute over the partial.** We respond to black-and-white issues much better than to gray ones.
- **The traumatic over the chronic.** A chronic condition, medically speaking, takes months or years to develop and appear. It builds up gradually, and often unnoticeably. Trauma is immediate and undeniable. Guess which one gets our attention?

- **The easy over the demanding.** Low-hanging fruit gets picked first. And why shouldn't it?
- **The contrasts over the similarities.** What stands out gets our attention. What blends into the background is overlooked. Business leaders "manage by exception," paying attention to things outside their plans.
- **The scarce over the abundant.** Scarcity implies value; obtaining scarce things confers honor, exclusiveness. Nothing is taken for granted more than the very air we breathe—until it is cut off. Then it gets top priority.
- **Want over need.** I saved this for last, but it's more than an afterthought in this list. It's huge, and we'll learn more about it in a page or two, when we follow a nude man into the woods.

Back to our monster-sized biases: simplicity and urgency. They're unmistakable and undeniable, like the cry of "fire!" in a crowded theatre. Crises get our attention. But step back a moment and remember that no matter what the current emergency, life will soon move ahead relentlessly. What is critical now will be trivial soon. What is latent (chronic) will appear and challenge us anew (traumatic). We can, however, learn from the past, and we can prepare for the future, despite our infatuation with the present. No matter how much the pace of life intensifies, we need not just cope with one day at a time. We need to live all our days, past, present, and future. Without an extended view such as this, we become slaves to what's current. We stunt our lives into a short interval unnecessarily, and we pay attention only to those who scream among us.

No human being should be forced to answer the question "What have you done lately?" Our lives each represent a story, and a good story has a beginning, middle, and end. No story is complete without all three. And all three belong to each of us. We should guard them accordingly.

The future, what is to come, seems to be the most privately guarded, the most treasured. Each of us *owns* our own future, an unlimited vista, a blank slate, empty canvas. And each of us dreams in it.

Step #4: DREAM—Lighting a Burning Desire. The first three steps of a great *Message* lead others to: (1) be interested in your message (Invitation); (2) respect you and allow you into their thoughts (Empathy); and (3) understand your message (Development). Stop here and you've achieved very little. Sure, you've enlightened others, maybe even taught them something they didn't know, but unless you get them to act on it, you're not compelling.

> Great dreams inspire great acts. Learn how to create and share them.

Corporate leaders call the Dream a *Vision*—an attractive end state, the goal of an ever-changing organization. Some are good at this, but many are terrible. The most common error is to assume that just because the boss wants something, the rest of the company feels the same way. This word *want* is important to the compelling. We need to explore *want* further.

The Dream step establishes *motivation* to think and act differently. Here your goal is to make them want something—not just know, understand, or appreciate it, but *want* it.

I need to make a major distinction now. *Want* is not the same as *need*. All of us need all sorts of things, all the time. But we don't act on what we need unless it's what we want.

Advertisers don't care if you need their products or not—their goal is to get you to want them. To them, success is getting you to want exactly what you don't need. People do what they want, regardless of whether they need it. Need is easily satisfied, want is insatiable. Build your dream with *want*, not *need*.

After all, hundreds of thousands of us don't flock to NASCAR events because there's an overwhelming social need to burn excessive fuel, wear out tires, employ drivers and pit crews, or make use of otherwise empty tracks. We flock to them because we want to. We want action, excitement, thrills. We want to identify with winning teams, to admire bold and skilled drivers. We want to be part of an event, a communal happening. We want to support and cheer on our heroes. We want to participate in the drama of it all. Joseph Knowles knew this as far back as 1913.

What We Can Learn From a Nude Man

"NAKED HE PLUNGES INTO MAINE WOODS TO LIVE ALONE TWO MONTHS"

That's the headline of the *Boston Post* on August 10, 1913. It seems that Joseph Knowles, a part-time illustrator and physical fitness buff in his mid-forties, proposed to set off, completely nude and unarmed, into the uncharted forests of northeastern Maine. He promised to live alone and take absolutely no equipment, maps, rations, or tools. On August 4, 1913, the day of his departure arrived. In full view of film cameras and reporters, Knowles shed all his clothes, smoked a final cigarette, shook a few hands, and walked alone into the bear- and cougar-infested wilderness to live, he boasted, "as Adam lived."

The whole affair was orchestrated by opportunistic newspaper publishers, eager to increase circulation by carrying the continuing story of Knowles' daring feat. As part of the caper, Knowles was to leave written progress reports at prearranged locations, telling of his exploits. These were duly collected, and daily updates kept readers across the United States riveted to the saga. Finally, the appointed day arrived for Joseph's return to civilization. On October 4, 1913, exactly 60 days later, as promised, Knowles emerged from the forest just south of Megantic, Quebec. And the press was there to record everything.

Striding proudly from a tree line, Knowles was surely a sight to see. Clad in a bearskin robe, the self-proclaimed "Maine Tarzan" was fit, healthy, and smiling. His feet were shod with handcrafted deerskin moccasins; he carried a bow and arrows and a knife made of dear horn. Knowles was an instant celebrity, pictured this way in dozens of newspapers across the nation. His tales of killing a bear with a sharp stone and wrestling a buck to death captivated everyone. (Later he had to confront the Maine Fish and Game Commission, which wanted to prosecute him for "hunting out of season!") Ahhh, the down side of fame.

Our "need" list is short. Our wants go on forever.

For 60 days and nights, Knowles lived and thrived in a complete state of nature—and with very minimal needs. He didn't need insurance, dental work, software, cologne, stocks, or anything else. Just the bare (bear) essentials. The point here is that if we really look at what we think we need with a jaundiced eye, if everything on

53

our need list is carefully evaluated, it would quickly shrink to a few readily available items. People need very little of what others try to sell them.

A postscript: Knowles created quite a controversy when his claims were examined. Seems his bearskin coat contained bullet holes, and out behind the makeshift camp he said he constructed, enterprising reporters discovered a pile of beer bottles and tin cans "about 4 feet high." Close, but not quite "back to nature." But hey, if a guy who has killed a bear with a stone and wrestled a buck to death doesn't deserve a few cold ones, who does?

Fear and Desire: The Prime Movers

Of all the motives that drive humans, fear and desire top every list. People move because they fear something (want to run *from* it) or desire it (want to run *towards* it). Of these two, desire is by far the most compelling. Fear works at times but it's often negative, seen as alarmist, and so very overused. Slant your Dream towards desire. Harness the latent expectations within others—the hunger they have to achieve, change, improve. You can salt in a little fear, but the main dish should always be desire.

The pinnacle of this principle—the absolute paragon of a compelling message—is Martin Luther King Jr.'s famous "I have a dream" speech. In it he drew a beautiful, alluring picture of a world yet to be. He painted this compelling canvas with glowing terms: respect, dignity, joy, pride, and justice. He could have resorted to fear—say by projecting a world of intolerance, racial strife, and inequality—but he wisely chose desire as the prime motivator behind his historic remarks.

> **Remember the past in black and white. Dream the future in color.**

The Dream step demands that you create a futuristic vision, a goal to be achieved, a new environment to enjoy. Something that pulls people toward it, tantalizes them, gets them excited and full of anticipation for what could be. Few of us are terribly compelled by a negative—what to fear, what can go wrong. We all chase a better future. With the Dream step, you offer an irresistible glimpse into it.

People Have Two Brains

Psychologists and neurologists have long contended that we have a bicameral (two-sided) brain.[4] The left side focuses on such tasks as mathematics, language, and logic. The right focuses on images, music, and feelings. Some people, the scientists tell us, have a strong left-brain orientation—these tend to be the ones studying and practicing engineering, accounting, the "hard" sciences. Those favoring the right brain are most likely influenced by art, color, sounds, shapes, impressions—the so-called "soft side" of life. To build an alluring dream, you need to hit both sides, right and left. Your vision of a compelling "to be" must cover this entire spectrum. Don't hammer on one or the other: hit both.

Never appeal to half a brain.

A few years ago, my wife and I decided to hire a general contractor to build a new home for us. At the initial meeting he did something quite remarkable. He pulled out blueprints to show that all our specifications could be met with his proposed design. There we could see the floor plan, foundation details, room sizes, and all the other components of our proposed dream house. It made a lot of sense, hit all the needs, was very logical. Then he pulled out an artist's rendition of the home. Here we saw a full-color rendering of the front of the place, complete with trees, flowers, a winding drive, and clouds and birds in the air above. I was sold right there.

"What does it matter by which wisdom each of us arrives at the truth?"

—Quintus Aurelius Symmanchus
(Roman Senator, 340–402 AD)

Message

I'm an engineer by training, so you'd think I'd be interested in the floor plans and blueprint details. No way. I was captivated by the image of this home, the thought of pulling into that welcoming driveway after a long day at work. The idea of bringing my friends over, showing it off. The pride I would take when realizing that this was really mine! I couldn't get the image out of my head. To hell with the details, the contract, materials, loan, interest rates, and construction schedule. I *wanted* this house! I could see it all right there, and I bought into the design immediately. My wife, on the other hand, was immersed in the layout, reviewing the traffic flow, room design, and kitchen workspace. I was hooked in the right brain, she in the left. We were compelled. We bought it and love living in it, each for our own reasons.

Components of a Real Dream

Only children believe in fairy tales, so make sure your dream is grounded, achievable. Strike a good balance between something one has to stretch for and something that's so easily attained it doesn't inspire. A general rule of thumb is this: If it takes longer than a year, it's viewed as too far off to drive action. Conversely, if it can be done tomorrow, it's not a dream, just a plan—a task on somebody's to-do list. To help you craft a compelling, actionable, and inspirational message, I'll quickly run through some do's and don'ts. Consider them a checklist you can use to build and review your Dream.

- **Does it seem achievable?** If your dream is a total makeover of world politics, the elimination of sin, or landing astronauts safely on Pluto, you're going to fail—and everyone knows this from the start. Don't deal in fantasy; deal in attainable goals. If you plan on embarking on a thousand-mile journey, start by imagining what the first ten miles will accomplish. Break long dreams into shorter increments—attainable ones. Compel people toward them, one at a time.

- **Can everyone understand it?** You must articulate the Dream in terms others can grasp, painting a picture they can comprehend. Use their words, not yours. Describe it simply and powerfully. Remember, the Dream is only a tool. Avoid complexity and intricate details. Sketch out the desirable future, don't design every aspect of it.

- **Is it challenging enough?** It can't be trivial or a slam dunk. It has to have elements of greatness and triumph. Management consultants call these "stretch goals." That's a perfect term.

- **Is it attractive to all parties?** Here's a common mistake made by people wearing business suits. They dress a dream in their clothing, and forget that most folks working for them wear other styles. A line worker couldn't care less about return on investment, capital management, or competitive advantage. He wants a better job, better pay, more security, a chance to grow and develop. Harness these wants. Tie them to the ones you have—show how they connect.

Once we get into our next change mechanism, *Reaction*, we'll discover how demanding this can be. We'll begin to realize that people have very different sensitivities, widely varying desires and values. What makes a 50-year-old white male jump for joy might not get a 20-year-old Asian female to bat an eye.

- **Is it too abstract to mean much?** I've heard many an organizational leader stress the need for lofty goals like "excellence," "quality," and "customer service." These are glorious abstractions—with the emphasis on *abstractions*. Question: How do we know when we are finally "excellent"? When do we hit "quality"? How much service does "customer service" require? Choose specific, tangible results instead. Things that can be recognized and measured. Everyone agrees we want a better world, but what does that mean? How do we know when we get there? What does it look like, feel like? Unless people can visualize living there, they won't be excited about getting to "there"—especially if the journey is a difficult one. No one runs after a concept—that's like trying to capture fog.

Only philosophers chase abstractions.

- **Is it forward-looking?** A dream can't be some version of "We're messed up and we're going to fix things." That may be your ultimate objective, to be sure, but it's focused on the past and the present. It leads to thoughts about what happened, why it happened. It leads to blame games and protective, defensive positions. Every dream must respect the past and even pay some homage to current accomplishments, but never dwell on them.
- **Is it catchy or memorable?** Every dream should be described in one or two sentences, or it's bound to be forgotten. Make yours short, crisp, memorable. That's why President Kennedy promised to "send a man to the moon and return him safely to earth before this decade is out." That's why Martin Luther King Jr. yearned for a future where his children were judged not by the color of their skin but the content of their character. These are powerful dreams spoken decades ago, but still remembered.
- **Does it try to be all things to everyone?** This requirement is a tough one. I've said the *Message* should be common, that everyone should get the same one. But just because the message is common, it doesn't have to solve all problems and please all people. If your dream is reasonable, it probably helps some people out more than others. Admit this and move on.
- **Is it backed up by a plan for accomplishment?** This is the final and most challenging test of all.

Once you've laid out your Dream, your next step is to demonstrate how to achieve it. This can't be left up to other people's imagination. You cannot simply lay out an attractive goal and expect others to fill in the blanks when it comes to getting there. You must answer the inevitable questions: What do we do now? Who does it? How do we do it?

One last point: If your audience is a tight group of like-minded members, say a club or association of people with the same interests, you can afford to craft a specific, detailed dream. It will hit them where they live—they'll relate to it. But if the group you're targeting is very diverse, consisting of people with little in common, you've got to use a more general dream, one based on universal principles or fundamental concerns.

This takes us to the final step—where action lives.

Step #5: CHALLENGE—Getting things moving. People who are compelling get others to think and act differently. Up to this point, our first four steps of a *Message* work on the initial task: thinking differently. This step takes us across the action barrier, where we want them not just thinking, but *doing*.

Your challenge is a roadmap to the future. It shouldn't stretch ahead to eternity—just the first few miles.

End every *Message* with a Challenge—a call to others, a dare, if you will. And it's either direct and specific or it's useless. But however you build this "to-do list," whether you're writing a sales proposal, talking with your children, or addressing millions on television, make one thing clear: *This is not going to be easy.*

Social historians often argue about what makes a civilization or nation succeed—what characteristics allow it to prevail over circumstances and other competitors. My favorite explanation comes from the great historian Arnold Toynbee in his masterwork A *Study of History*, written in 1933. In this 13-volume tome, Toynbee discusses the concept of *Challenge and Response*, of how certain societies respond to challenges, be they physical (drought, famine), technological (the Industrial Revolution), or invasions and wars: "In the history of civilizations, the interplay between challenges and responses is the factor which counts above all others—geography, race, history, technology, economy, and all the rest."[5]

According to Toynbee, this characteristic alone determines which civilizations thrive and which perish. When they respond to challenges, they prevail. When they don't, they fail. How's that for condensing 13 volumes into two short sentences? I believe Toynbee's conclusions also apply to individuals. It's not so much what you have, what you control, or even who you are as it is how you respond to the challenges you face. I also believe, and have seen this proven over and over, that all people welcome a challenge. However, it has to be the right challenge put in the right way. That's the next assignment for a compelling leader. And once again, it's not going to be easy.

You're up against a number of forces when you try to get others to move on your ideas—to act them out, make them real. Engineers refer to *static inertia*—the physical principle that things tend to remain as they are. The tendency is to stay at rest, whether we're talking about a 10-story building or a human being. And as Aristotle said "Nothing moves unless something pushes or pulls it." A good challenge has to overcome static inertia, get the wheels moving. Start slowly and build on the other type of inertia, what the engineers call *dynamic inertia*: the tendency to keep moving once a thing is set into motion. Toynbee wasn't writing about challenges alone in *A Study of History*. He was writing about *responses* as well. Challenges without responses are like questions without answers—annoying and worthless.

All effective change is made by individuals, for individuals.

You'll also confront resistance to change, apathy, a tendency to "let someone else do it." That's why your challenge must be personal. You must engage each individual into taking active steps. Organizations, companies, and even nations do not achieve dreams—people do. No great changes are made unless they are made by and for people. So don't end your *Message* with a collective call for change. Don't say "Our company will do this," without also saying "You, each and every one of you, must do this." Responsibility for change is a funny thing: When it's spread over a group not much happens—it's diluted and sort of evaporates. But when it's concentrated, when it's placed on individuals, stuff starts to happen.

If your audience, be it individuals or a group, has already done something that will help them take up or meet the Challenge, be sure to point this out. Confirmation of work already done and progress already made helps overcome static inertia.

Good and Bad Challenges

Here are a few examples to help round out your skill with challenges.

Situation One: You're addressing a community meeting to protest a zoning request. You want to activate fellow citizens against it.

Bad example: "Thanks for listening to my comments tonight. Now let's all get out there and fight this thing!"

Problems: Just exactly how are they going to fight it? Burn down city hall? Lie in front of the bulldozers? And who is supposed to do this? They'll walk away all fired up with nowhere to go and nothing to do.

Good example: "We need to enlist the support of everyone in this town to defeat this request. Many folks couldn't make this meeting, but they can help stop this. When this meeting breaks up, I recommend each of us here makes a list of five neighbors and calls them tonight. I'll create a petition and leave copies for you at the clerk's office. I'd like each of you to get five signatures on a petition. Pick them up tomorrow morning and leave them with your five signatures in my mailbox by Friday." This gives them individual tasks, a deadline, and the tool with which to achieve both. It is specific, measurable, and immediate.

Situation Two: Your daughter and her husband have been married for less than a year and already are up to their eyeballs in debt. They just can't manage their finances, and they've asked for your advice. You're on the phone with them.

Bad example: "Listen, managing your money is simple, really. All you need to do is spend less and save more. That's it—so get started!"

Problems: Even the village idiot knows what you've just told them. That's like saying to lose weight all you need to do is eat less and exercise more. If it were that simple, why are there so many financial advisors and weight loss clinics? You've scolded them but left them with no action items and no specific responsibilities. You've also washed your hands of them and their problems.

Good example: "Agreeing on your priorities is the first step, and I can help you get started. How about if I come by tomorrow and bring a worksheet we can complete together? We'll look over your expenses, sort your bills, and sketch out a simple budget for the next three months. If that sounds okay, put together your last month's bills and credit card statements tomorrow before I get there. How does 7 P.M. sound?" Here you've set a date, given them preparatory work, and outlined a short-term plan. You're also offering to roll up your sleeves and help.

Situation Three: You're the CEO of a big company that's just announced a merger with a competitor. You're addressing several hundred of your key managers in the corporate conference center.

Bad example: "I'm proud to announce our purchase of XYZ, Inc. This is truly a merger of equals, a win-win deal for everyone. Our stock has started rising since news of this got out. Wall Street embraces this strategic move. Let's face it, we're both in the same business, and combining our strengths is only natural. I want each and every one of you to stand behind me on this."

Problems: Everything about this challenge is wrong. You've trivialized the difficulty ahead, brushed aside the natural fears and anxiety every merger generates. You've underestimated the work involved and given no compelling reason for anyone to support it, much less any action they must take from here on out. In addition, you've cited Wall Street's reaction as a sign of success. But these folks don't work on Wall Street; they work here. The men and women in your audience aren't stupid or naïve. They know mergers often result in job loss, changes in power, reassignments, and more. By insulting their intelligence you've lost all credibility at a time when you desperately need it.

Good example: "We've decided to acquire XYZ, Inc. Even though the numbers tell a good story, all of us realize that making a deal like this is just the beginning. It won't pay off unless we succeed at integrating these two firms. And for that I need you. You make this company work and you are needed to make the combined outfit even better. Jerry is handing out a brief 100-day plan to you as I speak. Take it back to your offices and look it over. I've established a merger web site and selected ten integration team leaders. Many of you are now designated for one or more of these teams. Your job is to work with your team leaders to plan, and most importantly, execute a number of changes we must take to make this deal a success. It won't be easy and it won't happen overnight. It will require specific duties for most of you—duties beyond your normal operations. But no one is more capable of building a better company than you, the men and women who brought us to this point. I'm confident you will take us on to the next level."

This last one is a bit long-winded, but after all, you're the CEO.

Quick Tips for Compelling Messengers

Here are a few rules everyone should follow:

- **Memorable presentations are better than interesting ones.** Ask yourself: Of all I plan on saying, what will they remember most? Hint: They will remember you, your characteristics, your passion, and your stories long after they've forgotten your slides and logic.
- **What you believe, hope for, and aspire to are much more compelling than what you know.** Avoid phrases like "I think . . ." or "In my opinion . . . ." To be compelling you must *demand, believe, expect, support, fear, encourage, wonder, know, commit, pledge* — and not just think.
- **The more powerful a person, the fewer slides and shorter words he or she uses.**
- **Passion is good. Zealotry is bad.** Know when to quit beating the drum.
- **Compelling people speak and write simply.** You don't win when other people think you're brilliant. You win when they follow you.

Message

- **People welcome a challenge.** Everyone can easily become overwhelmed with choices and bewildered with alternative paths.

  In his classic work *Escape from Freedom*,[6] Erich Fromm reminds us that freedom of choice—the burden of making decisions—is not always positively viewed. Some, even many, actually dread it. They seek "escape" from this freedom. Having a plan to move forward liberates them from unfocused anxiety and undirected energy. Laying out a compelling *Message* can be immensely relieving to these people. Don't presume a challenge is dreaded, like some sort of onerous homework assignment. For a great number of us, it's welcomed.

Let's move into the next mechanism with a final note. Whether you're the community activist, concerned parent, or corporate chieftain, your job of compelling has now just begun. It doesn't stop here. You can't just inform, teach, and even motivate others if you want them to think and act differently. You've got to set up the tools they'll use, create the environment they'll inhabit, counter the resistance you're sure to confront, and enlist the aid of allies in this quest.

There are thousands of adolescent boys who would love to play on a professional basketball team. You can easily teach them the rules, instill a love of the game, and get them really charged up about the dream. But not a single one will make the pros if they're denied the training, support, diet, practice, encouragement, and permission this goal requires. Compelling others is not just about speaking or writing well. Delivering a *Message* is a good start. but it's not enough. You'll need to crank up more change mechanisms and develop more skills. You can find them in the next chapters.

Chapter 2

Reaction

> **re·ac·tion** \ rē-ˈak-shən \ *n*
>
> 1. A response to a stimulus.
> 2. The state resulting from such a response.

Funny how people who've never met or exchanged a word with each other react the same way to the same conditions. Like when the back door of an armored truck accidentally swings open on a city street, spewing bundles of cash in its wake. All of a sudden passersby take notice, and react the same way—they start to gather up the money gleefully. Businesswomen, barbers, paperboys, attorneys, beggars, hot dog vendors—all so different, yet all reacting the same. Funny how, given the right circumstance, the dignified and the disgraced, the diligent and the derelict—as if on command—all start diving for dough.

No one tells them what to do—they *know* what to do. Not a word is passed among them. But like dancers

in a carefully choreographed ballet, there they are—
stooping, bending, and scooping it up.

Or when a well-known citizen passes away and his
wake is held. All of a sudden, with no *Message*, no hidden director pulling the strings or calling the shots,
everyone who arrives at the funeral home is well
dressed. They're all quiet, full of dignity and respect.
They speak in hushed tones. They hug each other, nod
knowingly to strangers. They weren't told to do this.
They just do it.

Why do such different people react so uniformly in
different situations? Why do we trade one mode of behavior for another just because the scene changes? Why
are dignified university regents raving fanatics at football
games? Why do normal folks smile and bless one another in church, then give each other the finger on the
highway home?

For the same reason snotty-nosed eight-year-old girls
can pull the hair of their little sisters, and an hour later
appear on stage at a music recital as angels. For the same
reason bomber pilots can release carnage on cities one
day, then hug their children the next. A boxer can beat
the brains out of a colleague in the ring, then escort an
old lady across the street outside the arena. A judge can
relish the joy of mercilessly whipping a friend on the
tennis court, then shower, put on her robes, and grant
clemency to a murderer when she gets to the criminal
court. Even fish know this.

❏ Fish Don't Talk ❏

If you're fishing in the center of a shallow lake or stream on a hot, sunny day, chances are you won't catch many. That's because fish know the shady spots along the banks, and let the overhanging trees catch the heat of the sun while they cruise around coolly below. The chief fish didn't issue an order: "Okay everyone, it's getting towards noon. Head for the shore." No *Message* here—just *Reaction*. Each fish knows the difference between sun and shade, and when the former gets too hot, each heads for the latter. They don't pass the word around, don't chat it up. And chances are no fish learned this secret from parent fish. Parenting isn't high on the fish agenda. They just go where it's comfortable. Their environment guides their action.

The environment we're in dictates how we act.

While fish know this instinctively, it took university administrators a bit longer to catch on. You see evidence of this when a new set of buildings is constructed on campus. Architects lay out the sidewalks between these buildings in a typical rectilinear fashion. They prefer straight lines and 90-degree angles. Problem is, students prefer the shortest distance between two points when they're rushing from classroom to dorm, or gym to parking lot. So they cut across the lawns and, pretty soon, they've worn curving or diagonal dirt paths in the verdant fields of grass.

The authorities can post as many "keep off the grass" signs as they like, but then they've created a bigger problem: enforcement. Faced with this challenge, they've got to reexamine their objective. It isn't to keep students walking in straight lines—it's to keep them on the sidewalks, off the grass. So why not put the sidewalks where the students will walk? Why not alter the environment rather than trying to alter human nature? Put in sidewalks over the dirt paths—problem solved. Sure, these may not look as neat and orderly, but they work so much better. The objective shouldn't be rectilinear sidewalks. The objective should be students using sidewalks.

When you set out to affect outcomes, keep the environment in mind. It's seldom just a backdrop to action, an empty stage upon which your wishes are carried out. It's a key ingredient, an inseparable factor that will work for or against you. Compelling people know the environment is never a neutral platform. It is more often either an ally or an enemy. It can facilitate compliance with your wishes or frustrate and block it.

I'll use the term "environment" very broadly here. It includes physical settings, our surroundings, like the examples above regarding fish and students, but also much more. The environment includes all the behavior-shaping elements that surround the people you want to think and act differently. For employees this includes not just the physical workplace, the office, factory, and so on. It also includes their pay, working hours, equipment, reporting relationships, organizational structure, and the incentives and penalties affecting their jobs. For children this includes their homes, schools, neighborhoods, even the clothes they wear. For governmental leaders it includes the tax structure, legal system, and all the agencies and services provided to the public.

Frustration is the condition of holding new thoughts in an old world. And vice versa.

The *Reaction* mechanism requires you to know this environment and work within or around it—finding and removing obstacles to your goals and, at the other extreme, using *behavior enablers* the environment provides. In some cases, you will have to change the environment itself to fit your needs. But this should be the final choice. First use the enablers and avoid the obstacles that exist, and only then reach into the environment and make changes. Compelling people want to get others to think and act differently, not necessarily re-design the world.

In this chapter I'll describe how the *Reaction* mechanism works, and how you can use it to your advantage. This isn't a trivial concern. Some of the most articulate, motivating would-be leaders I've met have failed in this regard. Remember our definition of Compelling: getting others to think and act differently. Here we'll emphasize the "act" component. Regardless of how people *think*, of how they look at things, dream, and accept challenges, if you turn them loose in an environment that prevents them from *acting* differently, or punishes them when they do, you and they will fail together. "Acting" is the interplay between individuals or groups and their environment. To be compelling you must give equal attention to both. But first a quick story.

❏ Edwin Fails at Becoming a "Jock" ❏

Edwin (I'm using a fictitious name here, for reasons that will soon be obvious), one of my classmates in the eighth grade (we were about 12 or 13 years old), was shy and intellectual. He used large words, belonged to the chess club, and was eager to win acceptance by the rest of us guys. I suggested he try out for the school basketball team, and pointed out that this would build his self-esteem, diminish his egghead reputation, maybe even bond him to his cohorts. He reluctantly agreed and rushed home to announce this intention to his mother.

One of the school rules was that all boys had to wear an athletic supporter (jock strap) when competing in sports. Edwin's mother was a seamstress—she could make him one at home. So far, so good. The first day of practice, as we were all stripping off our clothes in the gym and donning our uniforms, Edwin pulls out this homemade jock strap. Mom had chosen a purple elastic fabric for the waistband (probably the remnant of a pair of her silk panties) and a bright red nylon sock for the actual "cup" portion. It was all so logical, inexpensive, well-constructed and functional, to be sure. But you can imagine the *Reaction* among this group of pre- and post-pubescent males! Sending Edwin into the locker room with that item was about as sensible as sending a lamb wearing a tutu into a den of wolves. Mom was undoubtedly a good seamstress, and a highly imaginative one at that. She just forgot about the environment.

❏ Humans: Animals that Make Models ❏

People who study what it is to be human, what separates us from the rest of the animal kingdom, often cite key distinctions: Humans use tools and animals don't (wrong—otters use rocks to smash open oysters; chimpanzees use twigs to fish for ants); humans communicate among each other and animals don't (wrong—birds, prairie dogs, and many others use alarms to warn each other of approaching predators); humans care for other members of their species and animals don't (wrong—ants sacrifice themselves for the defense of their nests), or humans look into the future and prepare for it (wrong—even squirrels do this by storing nuts for winter). You can take each of these and find many exceptions—instances where animals, in some way, do what humans pride themselves in doing exclusively. But to me there is one distinction that sets us apart from all creatures: We build and use mental models.

Want to change people? Change their model.

All of us carry around models in our heads. Our environments are just too complex and too fast-moving to do otherwise. We simply can't take in everything around us and consider all the millions of particulars, then formulate high-fidelity, "true" representations of it. Consider this: Chief Financial Officers of corporations don't actually manage *money*—they manage budgets and cash flow projections (models of money). Planners don't manage *time*, they manage schedules (models of activities and events). Human Resource executives don't manage *people*, they manage organization charts and compensation levels (more models). Athletic coaches don't manage *games*, they manage their lineups, plays, and training regimens (more models).

We must use models. These are simple representations of the world we inhabit and the rules that pertain to it—stick figures to mimic the key characteristics of whatever challenge we confront. Two things have to happen for each of us to be successful: (1) Our mental model of the circumstances we are in must match those circumstances; and (2) We must know the rules required to succeed in those circumstances. When either of these goes astray, we're in trouble.

❏ There Can Be Only *One* Napoleon ❏

When a person's view of the world is out of synch with reality, we call him or her abnormal, or disturbed, or just clueless. If you see visions, hear voices, believe everyone is out to get you, your model is a bit off-center, and you may be termed schizophrenic or paranoid. And believing in your low-fidelity model, you will probably take actions others view as inappropriate or strange. But to you, you're acting very appropriately—*and very logically.* After all, if aliens are trying to read your mind with x-rays, it makes perfectly good sense to cover your head with aluminum foil. According to your model and the rules that apply to it, you're simply being prudent. Your actions make sense, but they're based on a faulty model.

I once heard that the most logical people in the world inhabit mental institutions. "After all," a patient may pronounce, "I am Napoleon, so he [the real Napoleon of history] can't be Napoleon: *There can only be one Napoleon!*" Hard to argue with the logic. The mental model, however, is a train wreck. Counseling and medication seek to reorganize such an individual's mental model—to bring it into line with reality—and thus lead to more acceptable behavior.

So, when we see cash behind the teller window of a bank, our models of "bank" and "ownership" tell us to leave it where it lies—under penalty of law. Ten minutes later, when we see bank notes flying all over the street, our model of "free-for-all" and "finders keepers" tells us to grab as many as we can. Different reality, hence different model and different behavior.

> **Compelling is the art of realignment. Know why this is vital and learn how to pull it off.**

When we're in a cathedral, our models of "sanctity" and "worship" tell us to be solemn and quiet. Walking around the corner and entering a football arena, our models shift to "contest" and "conquer" and we start screaming for the home team and cussing out the visitors. Different model, different behavior.

The key point here is twofold: (1) Well-adjusted people have reliable models to match their environments; and (2) They adjust or revamp these models when their environment changes.

Whenever our models cease to reflect reality, the actions we take cease to be successful and can get down-right weird. This is like playing ice hockey on a basket-ball court. We may be superb hockey players, but trying to slap a puck up into the hoop won't win us many games. We need to realize this is basketball, and adjust our actions accordingly. This adjustment is called "alignment." We align our models with our actual circumstances, then align our actions with those appropriate models. This doesn't guarantee success, but it's a whole lot better than wearing ice skates onto the hardwood floor of life.

❏ My Trip to the Antipodes ❏

Ancient geographers called the Southern Hemisphere the *Antipodes*. This meant the exact opposite side of the earth. In the case of European cartographers, this meant way down south, below the equator. Today, *antipodes* also means two terms with "the exact opposite meaning." In the early 1980s I traveled to South Africa and experienced both definitions.

While on a lecture tour, I accompanied my sponsor and his clients to a rugby match in Johannesburg's newly opened Ellis Park Stadium. A crowd of us sat in a corporate suite in this magnificent venue to watch Transvaal take on Northern Transvaal. Waiters brought us succulent snacks and chilled cocktails as we watched the action below. I knew nothing of rugby and had no idea of the location, records, or players of either team, but on this exceptionally beautiful autumn afternoon in this magnificent, modern edifice, and after a few fresh prawns and some cold Castle beer, I was comfortably getting used to this experience. Then the match began.

After a few minutes of watching striped-shirted men run, hit, and hug each other in massive piles, I caught on that my new mates' team was Transvaal and started cheering their every move. I didn't understand the rules of rugby or know what geographic distinction could be made between Transvaal and Northern Transvaal, but my mental model of a sport match was going to suit me well. That is, until some chap from Northern Transvaal (the enemy) suddenly crawled out of a scrum and headed for the goal line. I started booing, but noticed quickly that my crew of clients was cheering him on! They were on their feet, applauding, and shouting out encouragement's like "Good show!" and "Wonderful play!" What didn't I understand—the team colors, the rules, what?

I thought I knew which team was which by then. And in *my* model of sports, you hate the opposition and love your team. They're bad, we're good. Seated in an American football stadium I would have been yelling things like "Kill him!" or "Rip his throat out!" Not here. They're cheering the enemy on! They're congratulating the team that is beating them!

The guys around me were operating on a model that

was antipodal, exactly the opposite. You see, to them the model of sport goes something like this: Sport is a field of endeavor where gentlemen strive to do their best, and when they do, we applaud them. My American, antipodal model went something like: Sport is where you hate and attempt to destroy the other team. I was in a new environment, and desperately needed to adopt a new model—one more appropriate, more fitting.

Models and the environment work either in alignment or opposition. And each affects the other.

A postscript: The very next evening I was invited by the owner of a diamond mine to attend the second inaugural event at Ellis Park Stadium: the much anticipated boxing match between an American (and black) world champion and a South African (and white) contender. Remember the era: apartheid. You would think the diamond mine owner, with a lot at stake in keeping things precisely as they were, and his entourage of lackeys would want the white homeboy to win. But no, not in the slightest. They were cheering the black American! But by then I'd changed my model to theirs: Applaud good sport, no matter the player. The Yank won, and all were pleased. Their goal was not to see their guy win—it was to see a world-class boxing match in a nation that had been sanctioned—put off-limits—by most international sports councils. They were elated at the opportunity to see the best in the business of boxing on their soil, in their new stadium. And these were big moneyed men who looked down on all the blacks in their world. Saw them as inferiors. Saw them as servants, maids, lawn boys. But the world of sport had special rules for them, regardless of the color barrier. Black servants need to be disciplined, brought into line. Black sport champions need to be celebrated. Seems counterintuitive, but we'll face this again and again. Different environments (sport vs. society in this case), dictate different behavior. This is a very important lesson.

❏ Who Cares about Models? ❏

Those who are successful at compelling others know this delicate interplay between people and their models. They know that, even for a two-year-old, learning a model and acting accordingly *works*. Got diapers on? Let your bladder and bowels loose whenever. Pretty soon, some kind adult will clean you up and install a fresh diaper. What could be better? Works every time. Now, when you start to toilet-train such a child, you're trying to get her to adopt a new model and a new way of succeeding within it. You're changing the model from "just let it go whenever you please—someone else will clean it up" to "hold it in until you are seated on a strange, intimidating device." This turns their whole world upside down. You're breaking the old rules—the ones they were born with. You're expecting them to adopt an entirely new worldview and alter their habits to fit it. All the ensuing trauma and resistance, the crying, control games, and defiance are just their way of expressing discomfort at this model disruption. Welcome to the task of getting others to think and act differently. These same reactions appear among grownups.

When you try to compel others to do something new, something untested and often risky, you've got to assume that they know their current world, have good models to represent it, and have honed the behavior that succeeds there. Unless you're dealing with the mentally disturbed (there are zillions of other books on this), you've got to assume you're dealing with adjusted people comfortable with their environments, their models, and their actions. Getting them to change one of these requires commensurate changes to all three of them. If not, if you fail at this, you're apt to cause tremendous confusion and resistance. Psychologists call this lack of alignment "dissonance." You don't want any part of it.

But it's bound to happen with even the simplest of changes, and you need to either eliminate it in advance or quickly deal with it when it occurs. Change the environment or the rules that work within it, and you must change people's mental models. Otherwise you're working against the law of *Reaction*. And *Reaction* almost always wins.

Before we get into how this is done, I've got to change a definition. Let's stop using this term *model* and start using *expectations*. Expectations are nothing more than models of what people want—models of what they expect in the present and into the future.

❏ Expectations Drive Reaction ❏

Check into any chain hotel in any city and you'll no doubt observe a big building, a welcoming lobby and registration area, banquet rooms, and a bank of elevators. Bellmen will be rushing about, toting luggage. Registration clerks will stand behind counters pecking on computer keyboards. Off to the side you'll find a bar and restaurant. Down a hallway, following the scent of chlorine, you'll no doubt discover an indoor pool and/or exercise room. Register, get your magnetic key, and take an elevator to your room. You'll find a bed, television, bathroom area, and perhaps a minibar. Pretty standard stuff. But you don't come to this place for that stuff. Not at all. You don't want it. You want something else.

You want security, peace, rest, entertainment, refuge, shelter. You want a place that meets these *expectations*. And your expectations drive your decision to stay or move on to another place. So you go through a quick mental checklist: Does this hotel meet my needs? Will it fulfill my requirements? You mentally map what they have against what you want. You map *things* to *thoughts*.

Lighting (thing) to security (thought). Restaurant (thing) to hunger (thought). Room (thing) to privacy (thought). Price (thing) to value (thought). Hotels sell things (buildings, beds, bars) and guests buy thoughts (security, peace, entertainment). This happens with every product and service you select, be it a home, car, or job.

> **The greatest ideas in the world often fail because they can't be mapped into expectations.**

I can't imagine the construction contractor erecting this hotel ordering a crew of workers to install more peace, move that entertainment, nail down that security. They don't think or work that way. They are providing things they hope will match your *thoughts*. And these two are felt and expressed in entirely different terms. If their things don't map into your thoughts, if the translation from things to thoughts is faulty, they lose your business. If you're building a future for others and you describe the things there, make sure they match their thoughts—their expectations. If not, you will also lose their business.

> **Hope is general.**
> **Expectations are specific.**

Check out any advertising pitch and see this trick played out. Want to sell a weight loss drink? Don't tout the can, the ingredients (things). Push the idea (thought) of becoming slimmer, fitting into a smaller dress size. Want to reorganize your company? Don't tout the new organization chart. Push the idea of more opportunity, better customer service, innovation. People in the marketing and sales fields have been using this transposition for decades. They know we don't buy a better camera—we buy crisper memories of Junior's fifth birthday party. We don't buy behemoth SUVs, we buy safety, "command seating." We don't buy cashmere, we buy "warmth without weight." They sell things, we buy thoughts. Carefully map what you propose against what they want. Compelling people have figured this out.

❏ Mastering the Reaction Mechanism ❏

So far we've discovered two keys to using the Reaction mechanism:

1. Environments influence behavior.
2. Expectations drive action.

Now it's time to investigate these more closely, with an eye toward affecting outcomes. First we'll cover them separately, so you can gain a keen understanding of how they can help or harm your cause. Then we will move on to the delicate interplay between them. You'll learn how to shape environments and shape minds. Mastering these two factors will bring you that much closer to becoming compelling.

Shaping the Environment

This lesson easily breaks down to two elements:

1. Pave the path.
2. Burn the ships.

Each has all sorts of ramifications, but here we'll cover the most important ones.

Pave the Path

Pave the path is a way of saying that you want them to succeed, you want to ease their transition from what they *currently* think and do to what you *want* them to think and do. Remember, you're not trying to test them or determine if they can make it to the future you prescribe. You're trying to get them to that future. So you want to do everything you can to help them. Pave their path. Remove the bumps and obstacles. Eliminate the detours. And smooth the way, grease the rails.

For most of his adult life, my father was an Army officer. He enlisted just prior to WWII, and after the war he immediately went to law school under the GI bill, tried his luck at private practice, then returned to the army as a JAG officer. So he dragged his wife and five kids around the world from assignment to assignment. When I was seven, we landed at Fort Carson, Colorado. Looking for some spending money, I found a barbershop there which allowed me to shine shoes. The proviso was that I would have to sweep hair off the floors every few minutes, but, hey, it was a place to work and ply a trade.

I fashioned a shoeshine box out of discarded vegetable crates, bought the requisite Kiwi polish and brushes, and set up shop among the barbers. Business was great! Dozens of soldiers, waiting for their haircuts, let me shine their combat boots at the outrageous price of 15 cents per pair. Having shined shoes was a big deal in the army then, with GI's getting kudos or punishment based on how well this was done. I knew how to do it, and flourished. These young men had a tough, demanding life. Shining their combat boots was one less thing they had to worry about. I made a little part of their world easier; I paved their path. If I were an adult, particularly one in power, I could have ordered them to shine their boots, inspected the result, ridiculed those deemed insufficient, maybe even held boot shining contests. And to what end? Leaders aren't here to test and admonish others. They're here to lead them to new worlds. They know this secret. Watch television and read newspapers and listen for the frequency of this notion. Compelling people make the future *easier*.

That's the magic word: *easier*. If I were to revisit my earlier rules for *Message*, in addition to "simpler is better" and "the present is more powerful than the past or future," I'd add this one: "Easier is better." Compelling people make it easy for others to succeed. You are not here to make their life harder, to test them, to see if they fail. That's for others, with other motives. The first rule of compelling others is: *You win when they win.* Do all you can to help them achieve your goals. It's that simple.

If it isn't easy and it's optional, many people won't do it.

When you aim to get others to try new ways of being, don't start by sending them into the woods, among the briars. Send them along smooth, paved paths. If the future you prescribe is an obstacle course, a place where all they know and hold dear is challenged, be prepared for a high dropout rate. Leaders with a high dropout rate aren't really leaders—they're losers. Shame on them.

Examples

Situation #1: Your 14-year-old son is shy, a bit of a loner. You believe this will handicap him during his developmental years. You've even considered sending him to a child psychologist, or some other sort of counseling. Why can't he fit in? And to top it off, he's campaigning for some ridiculous clothes that he claims "all the kids are wearing." This is the last thing you want to hear.

Bad example: The kid needs to get with the program. He needs to be more sociable, to fit in with the crowd. So what's his problem? You and your husband hate these clothes—they look terrible. Besides, you're saving for a new boat, and need to conserve cash. Once you have this boat, the entire family (son, sister, and parents) will be able to share some "quality time" on the weekends. And another thing: You and your husband came up the hard way—you wore what you could afford and didn't care what others thought. This is the price everyone pays for being an adult—he needs to learn the value of money.

Good example: Your son is in a precarious time— adolescence. You need to understand that peer pressure is huge for him. You must ask yourselves, what is more important: the "lesson" that what others think doesn't count, or a smooth, fairly painless time through the most difficult period of his life? Your son is more interested in establishing rapport with his contemporaries than spending some "quality time" with you and his little sister floating on some lake. Spend a few bucks and ease his transition into adulthood. Boat or no boat—letting him have some dignity and self respect won't keep you off the lake for a day. Paving the path means giving up some control. You and he will win in the end.

Sometimes you must give away control to *gain* control.

Situation # 2: You own a chain of auto repair shops, specializing in broken windshields. One of your subsidiaries distributes windshield wipers. And you've heard all about cross-marketing and add-on sales. Why don't your windshield repair shops carry and push wipers? After all, most people with broken windshields could also use a new pair of wipers.

Bad example: You issue a memo to all branch offices. From now on, each branch manager will be required to sell at least 10 percent of their monthly quota in wipers. That's it! They got the message, and they must comply.

Good example: You realize that extreme profit pressure on branch managers leads them to source wipers (even when they want to fool with them) at the lowest cost. Yet your intra-company accounting procedures require the wiper groups to reap at least a 25 percent margin on sales. So you've incented the wiper guys to keep their prices high and the windshield guys to get the lowest prices from outside vendors. No wonder they either screw the whole wiper idea or, when forced, buy wipers from your competitor. Make some changes here: Decrease the price of wipers to your windshield guys, and jack up the motives to your wiper guys for sending them on time, in the right way, to your windshield guys. Make it easy for both. You win when they win.

Situation # 3: You run a small, independent retail bank, and are having trouble competing with the big conglomerates. You notice that the man who services your air conditioning system at home wears a uniform, so does the guy who fixes your car, and the impression they give is very professional. Why not have your tellers and loan officers do the same? Why not upgrade your image? Get them to think and act differently?

Bad example: You issue an order Monday morning that, effective in two weeks, each bank employee must wear a uniform. But, you tell them, the good news is that you've arranged with a uniform supply firm to give them a discount. This change, you explain, will give the bank a professional appearance, and increase sales and please customers. Who could argue with that? In a few days, three of your tellers and one loan manager quit.

Good example: Your objective is professionalism, not the wearing of uniforms. You realize that this new requirement puts a financial burden on all concerned. They have to buy the uniforms and send them for dry cleaning—whereas they have been using their own clothes and washing them at home. You have two choices: Dump the uniform idea or pay the additional cost for your employees. If it's that important, pay for it yourself. If not, forget the idea. Spend the money on training instead. Customers don't care so much that their bank tellers wear uniforms as that they care about their accounts and treat them with knowledge and courtesy. You want your people to help you grow your business—not to look like they're in the military.

It's All in Execution

These bad examples, though different, have one thing in common: You start with a good idea (more sociable son, cross-selling of wiper blades, professionalism among bank employees) and blow it in the execution stage. You place obstacles in the path of people you want to think and act differently. Well, some may say, that's their problem, not mine. No, no, and no. That's your problem, not theirs. You may be *right*: Junior may need some self discipline, the windshield guys may need to think big and consider corporate profits, and the bank employees may need to be more professional. But none of this will happen when you place obstacles in their paths. Being compelling isn't at all about being judged *right*. It's about affecting outcomes. And outcomes occur during the execution stage. Pave the path. Make it easy for them to win—not in the idea stage, but when things really have to change. Many of us can agree with an idea; that's easy. Few of us can get others to pull it off.

Compelling people never engage in zero-sum thinking.

Another way to think about this is that you want an environment that pulls others into doing what you wish, not one that pushes them away. So to get what you want done, you'll need to overcome these common obstacles—these roadblocks on the paved path.

Common Obstacles You Can Blow Away

1. **You don't do it.** Delta Airlines, while sliding into bankruptcy, was negotiating with their pilots union, seeking salary concessions—trying to save a few bucks. At the very same time, they were awarding huge bonuses and severance packages to the top executives who got them into that mess. Kind of stupid, don't you think? I put this obstacle up front because it, and all its variations, is so prevalent. If *you* don't change, how in the world do you expect others to? We're going to dive into this deeply when we come to the "Witnessing" mechanism in a later chapter. Quick preview: Leading means going first, taking the hits. It means doing—not just telling. You are the greatest advertisement for what you propose. Leading is "show" business, not "tell" business.

   Want your children to read more? Do it yourself—and make sure they see you doing it. Want them to stay away from the TV? Do it yourself. Want them to lay off junk food? Push that plate of cheese nachos out of *your* reach. Leading isn't easy. But unless you set the example, it's just blah, blah, blah.

2. **They don't have the tools.** Give them what they need to succeed. Give them the tools, information,

and most importantly, the permission, to carry out your wishes. If they have to go find them, buy them, or steal them, chances are they won't. Make it easy. Remove the "but I don't have . . ." excuse.

3. **You want them to draw a square circle.** Don't allow conflicting priorities. If you're running an on-call tech representative service, and your boss is pushing carpooling—Uh-oh! He's telling them to carpool and you're telling them to be flexible, work swing shifts, crank up their personal cars and go to the customer, whenever. Doesn't match. Decide what you really want—a square or a circle. You can't have both.

4. **They're just beaten up.** You keep piling on new requirements, new rules, new targets. Humans can only take so much change, then a phenomenon called "change fatigue" sets in. They've had it—they can take no more. Or, more commonly, they start calling your new crusades the "flavor of the month" and treat them accordingly. Select your battles carefully, and don't push beyond the threshold of human tolerance. Sometimes you have a great idea that has to wait—until they are settled in and can adapt to something new. Push too much, shove too many changes down their throats, and sooner or later they'll break. Pace yourself, temper your expectations with reality.

5. You pay for disobedience. Hard to fathom, but also common. You ask them to do X and your pay scale rewards them for doing Y. You want your customer-service associates (the men and women who answer the customer calls) to be friendly and helpful, to listen and show courtesy—yet you measure them on length of calls. You reward those who spend the least time with each call. "Wow!" you announce to them at the weekly review meeting, "Angela beat the record. She spent, on average, only 12.5 seconds with each caller. She's the greatest!" Can't have short calls and listen to the customer. Take your pick. You can't have both. There are two truisms in management: (1) You get what you pay for; and (2) What gets measured gets done. Make sure they're "aligned."

Never expect X and encourage Y.

---

6. Are we there yet? Everyone with children has heard this refrain from the back seat on every long-distance car trip they've ever taken. Children have to ask it— they can't read maps or calculate distance, much less forecast ETA (estimated time to arrival). Heck, even airline pilots have trouble with this. Adults, as sophisticated and experienced as we may be, still have the same question: What is our intermediate progress?

How much more do we have to go? Never send others out on a journey without providing them with milestones: measures of intermediate progress. All of us need reassurance: Are we getting closer? This is another execution challenge: providing others with confirmation that this new thing works, that this journey is progressing. Give it to them.

In the late 1970s and early 1980s, a strange phenomenon took place in the realm of long-distance running. Across the world, times to run every distance started to shorten. Runners were getting faster, records were being broken. What was causing this quantum improvement? Was it better training? Improved diet? Evolution?

Nothing of the sort. It was *feedback*. And it happened with the invention of a cheap, black plastic wristwatch. While training, runners had instant access to their progress. All they had to do was glance at their wrists and see how well they were doing. No coach on the sidelines thumbing a stopwatch and hollering out times. No need for that. Just look at the digital readout at selected points and compare the time with your expectation. Behind schedule? Better put on the speed. Ahead? Better slow a bit and pace yourself. Runners took all this into account while training and while competing. Times got shorter. Speed increased. More than better diet, more advanced clothing or better shoes, knowing how one was doing, while it was ongoing, spurred improvement.

Intermediate results spur continuing effort.

Everyone wants to see the fruit of their labor—as early as possible. We all, marathoners and the rest, need to know, "Are we there yet?" Pushing others to do something different requires you to provide this. Let them know if they're meeting expectations. And, for goodness sake, do this while they are *on* the journey—not when they've either failed or succeeded—that's too late. You don't compel at the start of the race, then sit back and see what happens. *You* are the wristwatch, the timing mechanism. You shout encouragement and corrections all along the path.

Burn the Ships

Warning! This story may be *apocryphal*: That means we're not sure it is true. But it sounds true, and means a lot to would-be leaders. So let's take it as far as it goes.

In the summer of 1519, after several preliminary landings and encounters with fierce, warlike inhabitants, Hernan Cortez beached his fleet of ships at Villa Rica de la Vera Cruz in what is now Mexico. Bent on conquest and gold, these conquistadors had heard of the mighty Montezuma and his nation of Aztec warriors some distance inland. Members of coastal tribes, enemies of the Aztec, told frightening tales of them. They wielded obsidian-tipped war clubs so as not to kill, but maim their opposition. This because the Aztecs took captives to the top of their stone-stepped pyramids (teocalli) and butchered them alive—cutting out their still-beating hearts as tribute to Aztec gods. Others they boiled alive or grilled, and ate. Next to one teocalli in their capital city, escaped prisoners recounted, stood a huge pile of skulls—over 180,000 in all.[1] And it wasn't unusual, on holy occasions, for more than 10,000 sacrifices to take place on a single night. Not the stuff to inspire your average foot soldier thousands of miles from home, eating strange food and sweltering in armor under a tropical sun.

A huge battle with the Aztecs was imminent, and Cortez wanted to steel his men to the fight. He ordered his ships burned (or dismantled, depending on the version read), to prevent them from sailing back to Cuba. Once this was done, they were committed—conquer or die, no escape. This legend has led to the expression "burn the ships" to describe a "no turning back" situation.

Variations on this notion take the form of "burn the bridges to the past," "the burning platform," and many others. Funny how they all seem to use the fire metaphor—a dramatic way of indicating complete destruction of the way things used to be.

When you compel people into a new way of thinking and acting, you are, in a way, sending them across an ocean of uncertainty to an unknown land. Allowing them an escape route, most commonly a way back to their old world, is full of risks. The temptation to revert, backslide, or just quit and return to conditions as usual is tremendously appealing during times of uncertainty. If you can eliminate this option you have a much greater chance of success.

A more contemporary example is the conversion of a traditional business process to an automated, or even web-based one. Information systems experts learned years ago that there needs to be a "conversion" date—a time when everything has to shift from "the way we've always done it" to the new way. Allowing a gradual shift, a phased transition, seems to make sense. After all, it gives folks time to test and adjust to the new system. But it also carries the risk of reversion, of abandoning the new during the trying startup sequence. That's why they began to insist on a "no turning back" conversion. They decommissioned the old equipment, retired the programs on that date. They burned the ships. To extend the nautical analogy, conversion day marked the point of no return. It works, and is now accepted protocol. System architects wouldn't think of doing it any other way.

Push past the point of no return.

❏ **Moveable Feast** ❏

In Christianity, a *moveable feast* is a holy day whose date is not fixed to a particular day of the calendar year but moves in relation to the date of Easter, which itself falls on a different date each year according to a specific formula. Fixed holidays, like Christmas day, are always on the same date (in this case, Dec. 25). So if you ask anyone which date Christmas falls on next year, you're apt to look quite dull. Yet ask any person for the date of next year's Easter, and they'll start guessing or searching for a new calendar. When compelling others, you don't want any questioning—any adjusting. Stay far away from the moveable feast notion. Pick and announce fixed dates—real datelines are magnificent ways to get things done. Eliminate the tendency to slide that date forward, and don't aim for some vaguely chosen time off in the future. Deadlines drive action.

A deadline is a leader's best friend. Pick a good one.

You'll see this in Christian nations during the latter part of December, all the way up to Christmas Eve. The shopping centers and malls are packed. If you're brave enough to visit them then, you'll also see folks that look like they just crawled out of caves for the first time in a year. The most infrequent shoppers simply have no choice—the deadline of Dec. 25 is nondebatable. They have to get Aunt Alma a gift—no way out of it. Deadlines drive the most recalcitrant among us to get off their cans and do what must be done. Use these dates wisely, however.

Make sure they're reasonable, achievable. Don't say, "By sundown tomorrow, I expect you to lose 30 pounds." Or, "When this pack is finished, I will officially quit smoking." That pack will grow and multiply for months. Or "Beginning next Monday, we will be the most customer-driven tire store in the city." The obvious question then becomes "Just how do we know when we're the most customer-driven store, anyway?" This last example leads us to one of the biggest mistakes you can make: setting a goal that cannot be quantified, can't be measured. You never know when you're there.

Can I Touch It?

You want goals to be tangible, ones that self-identify. You want to be able to say, with certainty, we've achieved it— we're there. And you want to publicize intermediate progress all along the way to reaching those goals. That's why astute leaders almost always choose real, measurable outcomes. Something you can touch, see, weigh, count, say is here or isn't here.

> **What gets measured gets done.**

This means you don't tell them you want them to plan (verb). You tell them you want a specific type of plan (noun) on a specific date, and that it should contain these specific elements. Otherwise you'll walk into a conference room full of charts and reports and spreadsheets, with people hunched over them, scribbling and debating away. "What's up?" you'll ask. And they'll tell you, "We're planning." Come back six weeks later, ask the same question and get the same answer. Planning doesn't buy you a thing, it doesn't get you higher performance or better sales or more customer service. "Planning" is an activity—not an outcome. *Compelling leaders want outcomes*—real plans they can use, ones they can "touch."

❏ Shaping Minds: The J-Curve ❏

In August of 1961 I was the first person in my neighborhood to know of one of the biggest events of my generation. I was a paperboy, and in the pre-dawn darkness I bent over my freshly delivered bundle of newspapers with a flashlight and pair of wire snips. The bold, large print headline of the top paper grabbed my attention:

COMMUNISTS ERECT WALL IN BERLIN. There, in a grainy black and white photo, were two East German border guards slapping mortar on concrete blocks separating "free" West Berlin from communist-controlled East Berlin. No symbol could better evoke the separation of global ideology and geopolitical intent than this.

The J-Curve built this wall.

In November of 1989 the wall came tumbling down. Democratic movements, supported by millions of people behind the Iron Curtain yearning to be free, overcame their totalitarian governments, and the Soviet satellite nations fell like dominoes, almost overnight. The wall had stood for 28 years, but it could stand no more.

The J-Curve tore down this wall.

The J-Curve will be your ally or your enemy. To become compelling, you should learn how it works, otherwise it will work against you. James C. Davies came up with this particularly telling theory about rising expectations and the likelihood of massive social movements back in the 1950s. He devised a simple representation of the force behind many revolutions and other dramatic social changes, and it became known as the Davies J-Curve. It fits all sorts of situations—involving nations, communities, and individuals equally because it explains *how the power of unmet expectations* comes about and what it can do.[2] Let's take a look at this, as shown in Figure 2.1.

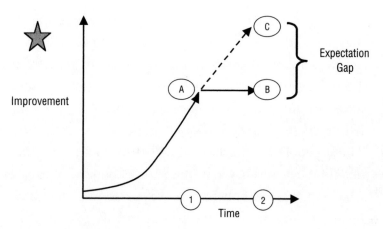

Reaction

Figure 2.1 The Davies J-Curve

The basic idea is this: Over time, most people's expectations tend to rise, like the line that moves upwards from virtually no improvement to points A and C. They *expect*, hope, pray that their living conditions will improve—things will get better. When this doesn't happen, when their actual conditions start to taper off, flatline, or even decline (shown by the horizontal line segment A-B) frustration sets in. People look around at what they have and notice it falls short of what they expected to have at that time. This difference is termed the *Expectation Gap*. When the Expectation Gap gets intolerably large, stuff starts to happen. People start to think about alternatives they may never have considered before. Dissatisfaction with the status quo increases quickly, the energy for change grows—and it can reach explosive levels. This

109

tension is dangerous for those wanting to keep things as they are, and it's a gift for those who want to compel.

Remember this: No one changes if everything around them is perfect. Their lives are comfortable, they have no unmet needs or hopes, and they resent anyone telling them that they should think or act differently. These people cannot be compelled to do anything but defend what *is*. They can never be energized to create what *isn't*. They simply have no Expectation Gap in their heads. If you want to move them, you have to *create* that gap. You have to show them either: (1) What they have isn't so cool after all (devalue their present condition); and/or (2) What they could have is fantastic (jack up their expectations). You fight inertia this way—by stretching that Expectation Gap (points B to C on the graph) as much as you can. Only when it reaches a certain level will the actual pain of the present become unbearable and the potential gain in the future become compelling.

Big change doesn't start at the top or bottom of society. It starts with people whose actual conditions don't meet their expectations.

So when the East German government built the wall in 1961, everyone thought it was to keep their people in—to block their escape to the free world. Actually, it also *kept the free world out.* It kept their people from seeing what "could be," what they "could have." They wanted to shrink the Expectation Gap by lowering point C and convincing citizens their actual conditions at point B were higher than they really were. They did this with propaganda on how poorly the West treated citizens, showing homeless and unemployed people, crime, chaos. Then they heralded conditions on their side of the wall. Wow, they repeated in state-controlled newspapers, television, and radio, we've never had it so good.

Only when the citizens of the Soviet bloc started peering over the wall at the other side did they realize how high Point C actually was and how low Point B had slid for them. They picked up television shows from the West and saw the homes, cars, and fun everyone was having there. They tuned in to rock music and news reports and learned two things: (1) The other guys have it pretty good; and (2) We suck. The rest is history.

To keep things as they are, people in power compress the J-Curve—they don't want the energy for change, the dissatisfaction, to grow this way. To get others to think and act differently, compelling people do the opposite—they stretch it out—make it very visible and constantly remind them how much difference there is between where they are and where they could be. This *Reaction* is not to be ignored. Unmet expectations represent a power tool—and like all forms of power, it can be used for good or evil.

**No Expectation Gap,
No change.**

Marketers know this quite well. Notice how many advertisements tell you (better yet, show you) how your life *could* be so much better if only you buy their product. How you *could* be attractive, socially in-demand, if you simply color your hair. How you *could* be a well-paid and influential executive if only you enroll in their MBA program. How you *could* become a better lover if only you buy Viagra. How you *could* rest well each night and greet every morning full of zip if only you down their sleeping pills. And, of course, how you *could* pay less taxes, drive on better roads, and enjoy excellent schools if only you vote for this politician. Most use a cunning bit of trickery with this. They show you a huge Expectation Gap, and imply that you can move across it with just one simple, easy step (*their* step). The unspoken message: Big gain for tiny pain.

Another apocryphal story. A large international conglomerate wanted to establish production facilities in a remote, underdeveloped part of the world. They had trouble convincing the locals to sign up for jobs in their mines, mills, factories, or whatever. These subsistence dwellers saw no need for work of this type. And money? What was money to them? They gathered their food from nearby forests, fished in ancient streams, built their dwellings from locally available, and free, materials. Why should they care about money? Then some genius decided to raise their expectations a bit—to create an Expectation Gap. Soon planes were circling the native villages, air-dropping Sears, Roebuck catalogs. Here they saw wonderful, enchanting appliances, tools, toys—all the largesse of the industrial age. According to the story, they started lining up at the hiring office. They couldn't wait to make this new thing called money, because money could buy what they never before knew existed, but now wanted badly.

Because of its power and universality, the Expectation Gap can be abused and misused, and it often is. Just because it *can* work for you doesn't mean it *will*. Time for some tips.

Tips and Tricks for Exploiting an Expectation Gap

1. **Some people have Expectation Gaps and don't recognize them.** Or they can't picture or articulate them. Your job is to surface one and demonstrate how real it is and how capable they are of closing it. This is why many proven programs for uplifting

poverty-stricken kids involve a summer camp away from the ghetto. A time to see and experience how well and happily others live—and most importantly, *how they could live* if only they stay in school, don't get pregnant, or stay off drugs. Without this exposure, many of these disadvantaged children might never imagine a different life, much less expect to achieve one. This glimpse "over the wall" is intended to make what they *could be* real, attractive, and most of all achievable—in short, compelling.

2. **Don't assume the gap exists.** It may not—they may be perfectly satisfied. I was giving a speech to a group of oil company executives when I learned this one. They were all seated in a Houston conference center, with the big bosses arrayed across the first row of seats. There they were, right up front: the CEO, COO, CFO, CTO, and all the other C-something-Os in the corporation. Behind them, in successive rows probably indicative of the corporate pecking order, sat their underlings: Division, Regional, and Department Managers, about 200 in all. To introduce the Expectation Gap concept I asked the crowd a question. "How many of you," I asked, "would like to have the exact same job as you hold today 10 years from now?" Hoping no hands would rise, I should have known better. All hands went up in the first

row, and only the first row. When you're trying to initiate a change in the ways things are done in a group, be careful with the guys in charge. They've got a lot to defend and little to gain. The way to energize these is to point out how much better their competitors are doing, and how the gap between their group and the others is widening. The bad guys are pulling away. Better get moving, or you'll be left in their dust. MBA-types call this "Competitive Strategy." They've got all sorts of associated buzzwords, like *best practices, best-of-breed, business intelligence, world-class,* and *benchmarking,* with shelves of books on each. I call it wanting to beat the bad guys. Simpler is better.

3. **Break the gap into smaller pieces.** Got a long journey ahead? Take it one step at a time. As each step is made, shout encouragement and accomplishment. Look for and celebrate "easy wins," the small, yet tangible evidence that things are progressing as planned. When they're struggling and striving, remind them of the ultimate dream. Dreams are great when it comes to getting started. They're even better at mid-journey.

4. **Everything is nigh.** This is a wonderful word that most Americans don't know and all British do: *nigh.* It means the same thing with relation to time that "near" means to distance—almost there, close, just

about. All people working to make things different need to be reassured that the end is nigh. You hear this when a parent is cheering on a child at a swim meet: "Keep going Jason, you're almost there." Who gets motivated by "You just started—there's one hell of a long way ahead"? When success is nigh, most people will go for it. If it isn't, they may not. Another reason to break long changes into increments that are always nigh.

> **When success is within reach, most people extend their grasp.**

5. **Expectations are moving targets.** They change, they differ among individuals. Don't push expectations simply because you have them—others might not. They may have entirely different views of the future, different values, and different needs. Find these out in advance. If they are too diverse, reach down to more common ones. That's why I call this mechanism *Reaction*. It's the infrastructure of behavior, the common ground.

That common ground can often be shaken, even turned upside down. Despite your best efforts, it is not always envisioned and designed by you. Other forces and

factors are at work, ones you may have trouble control-
ling. But just because you can't control them doesn't
mean you can't take advantage of them. This is a good
time to shift our perspective—to move from the view-
point of one wanting to compel others to those "others"
themselves. Let's stand for a moment in their shoes. See
what else affects them. The next change mechanism,
GroupThink, does just that.

Chapter 3

GroupThink

> **group·think** \ ˈgrüp ̄ˌthiŋk \ *n*
>
> The act or practice of reasoning or decision-making by a group, especially when characterized by uncritical acceptance or conformity to prevailing points of view.

D espite the inconvenience and hassles of business travel, one aspect is extremely interesting, at least to me. When you spend years travelling weekly to big-city hotels, you discover the most amazing groups holding conventions. Seems every conceivable topic, hobby, and profession has its own association, and they like to gather together, rub shoulders, exchange stories. There's a group for everything, even things you can't fathom. People who collect Jim Beam whiskey bottles. Folks who wholesale soybeans. Fellow travelers who seek their inner children, shampoo African cats, race vacuum cleaners. You name it, no matter how strange and off-beat, any conceivable topic, cause, or fetish, and there's a group for it—with members who just love meeting and hanging out with like-minded aficionados. In their normal settings back home, each may be deemed an eccentric, even a weirdo. But group them together in a community of shared interest, put them in a hotel ballroom among their peers, they're no longer outsiders. They suddenly *belong*.

These are people who seem to live an oxymoronic life: They want to be different, distinct—yet they love clustering with others of the same persuasion. Here's that same conundrum we encountered in Chapter 1 dealing with Empathy: *Like them yet unlike them*. We all share this split personality.

Even the staid business world has these groups, and the money (or expense accounts) to pursue them. Each gathering seems to have its own slogan—sort of a theme for the convention, conference, or symposium they've organized. These can be quite oxymoronic too. I've seen banners at these fests with slogans like "A Bold New Tradition," "The Leadership Committee," and "the First Annual such-and-such." But one that stands out in my memory was contrived by a group that should have known better. They met in Tucson, Arizona, and invited me to give the keynote speech. For anyone who has to speak in public, who needs to get a message across to strangers, this promised to be a supreme challenge. The group was the Public Relations Society of America—the men and women who run big PR firms and represent politicians, celebrities, public corporations. I was a bit intimidated; these were the top professionals in the world of communications, buzz, spin. I flew in the night before, and woke up in the hotel quite early, unable to sleep any longer—too nervous. This would be the Olympics of public speaking. Flashbacks of gravel parking lots and flatbed trucks spun through my mind.

But when I walked up to the stage that morning, I felt a little better, a bit more relaxed. For even these pros were meeting under an oxymoronic banner. Across the wall behind me was a huge sign proclaiming "Welcome to the *Renegade Rendezvous!*" I stifled a chuckle, realizing that even the best and the brightest in this messaging game had come up with such a silly concept. After all, *renegades* are those who flee from a crowd—who run out into the wilderness to be alone—ones demanding to be different. And a *rendezvous* is a gathering of people with something in common. You can't have both, I smugly concluded. Even the PR champs had fumbled here.

In important ways, we are all renegades looking for the right rendezvous.

But had they? Was it possible they were way ahead of me in their thinking, and knew something I didn't? Could *Renegade Rendezvous* have a special meaning, maybe one only those few among us understands? Only after a lot of thinking, reading, and reflecting on the nature of things did I come to the conclusion that they *were* onto something. They were right. We all want to be individuals, and we all desperately need to be a part of something bigger than ourselves. We all live this oxymoronic life. We are born loners, knowing nothing and no one. Then we encounter *GroupThink,* and it has a huge role in our lives. Compelling people cannot ignore Group-Think. It's all around us; it's alluring and powerful. We must learn to recognize it and harness it to our cause. Otherwise we'll be nothing but a voice with no listeners, an unread banner on the wall of an empty auditorium.

I thank Erich Fromm for this apt quote: "The fact that utter failure to relate oneself to the world is insanity, points to the other fact: that some form of relatedness is the condition for any kind of sane living."[1]

❏ The Thicket of Social Norms ❏

I use *GroupThink* to represent that thicket of social influences that guide individual sentiment, and hence, behavior. The pressures and attractions of that thicket are complex and interacting. They reinforce and contradict each other, pushing and pulling us into all sorts of conflicts and dilemmas. And no one is immune. The thicket engulfs us all, and it's alive. It grows in new directions, shrinks in others, constantly shifting—gaining and losing force over the long term, and in some cases, almost instantaneously. We can't cover it all, and no one can presume to understand it all. It's just too intricate and thorny.

> **The tangle of social influences has two elements: *me* and *them*.**

But we all live within it, the compelling and the compelled. Everyone you wish to affect is there, in that thicket, among the flowers and the thorns.

It's been said that all philosophy is but a mere footnote to Plato, the ancient Greek scholar. That may be true, but I have another definition that will help us navigate the thicket. I believe that all philosophy, religions, systems of belief, and cultural norms exist to answer two fundamental human questions: (1) Who am I?, and (2) How do I fit in with my world? These two intertwining concerns are the taproots of the social thicket we inhabit. They will guide us through the undergrowth of cultural influences.

❏ An Army of One? . . . Duh! ❏

As I write this the U.S. Army is experiencing its worst recruitment shortfall in 26 years. In the 12-month period just ended, their goal was 80,000 recruits and they came in 6,627 shy. Month after month, quotas for new enlistees are missed, and missed significantly. This despite a tremendous push from the Pentagon to beef up the effort of attracting young men and women into the service. More recruiters have been assigned, more spent on advertising, more networking with those who influence adolescents (high school teachers, coaches, ministers, scout leaders, and so on), and ever-growing bundles of cash bonuses and training promises to entice them into the military. It just isn't working. The ranks are thinning, and even those whose term of enlistment is up are forbidden from leaving. The Army has issued a "stop-loss" order to slow the discharge of current soldiers who would, under normal recruiting conditions, be readily replaced.

Commentators point to a number of factors: daily news of casualties in the Middle East, growing job opportunities in the civilian sector, a post 9/11 drop-off in patriotism. They're probably right; all these are having an effect. But I have to believe that their recruiting slogan is also partly responsible. For the generation they are pursuing, the age group they're chasing, "An Army of One" is about the worst campaign message they could ever have dreamed up. Might have worked for the Vietnam era, when young men and women were determined to be individuals, to split from conformity, tune out, to "do their own thing." But that was decades and two generations ago. This new crop of citizens lives in an entirely different thicket.

It goes without saying that different age groups respond to different conditions. Teenagers are driven by different factors than geriatrics, infants than the middle-aged. That's pretty basic. But another phenomenon is less understood: Different generations respond *differently at the same stages of their lives.* Today's over-60 crowd thinks and acts, on the whole, entirely differently than the same age group 50 years ago. Back then they were sitting in rocking chairs or lying in cemeteries. Now this same age group is swinging clubs on the golf course and swinging at Club Med. They're not pulling down scrapbooks of faded photographs, they're pulling down one-armed bandits and throwing dice in Las Vegas. Same with every other cohort group, including the Army's target market. Teenagers now are interested in and driven by very different factors than their parents and grandparents *when they themselves were teenagers.*

Different generations inhabit different social thickets.

No one saw this playing out better than two social commentators who wrote a brilliant book on the topic, one on my top-ten reading list of all time. It's *Genera-*

tions, by William Strauss and Neil Howe.[2] These guys cracked the code on behavioral mega-shifts, found patterns, and lay out a basic premise: There is a recurring flow of generational types over time, with a set of four basic models that repeat themselves in a particular sequence. They tracked them over hundreds of years of American history, and forecast the ones to come. To me, they nailed it.

One of these four recurring generational types they call the "civics," and the current set includes those born after 1982. This is the target group for our military recruiters—with the eldest now turning 25 and the youngest still in grade school. "Civics" tend to value community over individuality, responsibility to group over "finding oneself." In their rising adulthood (age of military availability), they "develop activity-oriented peer relationships, peer-enforced codes of conduct, and a strong sense of generational community. They band together at a historic moment . . ."[3] They don't want to be an Army of One. They want to be an Army of All.

The previous round of civics happens to be what Tom Brokaw called "The Greatest Generation," the GIs who fought in WWII. That is a group that cheerfully joined a cause larger than themselves, loved wearing uniforms, joined the veteran's clubs, filled Elk and Moose lodges, and fought a generational battle with the

non-conforming, individualistic children (their children) of the 1960s. As for the great questions of "Who
am I?" and "How do I fit in with my world?," this group
focuses exclusively on the second question. To them,
group identity *is* self-identity. To them, and to our current crop of civics, an Army of One is not only an impos-
sibility, but anathema. A new generation inhabits a
different thicket. It's driven by different needs and cher-
ishes different outlooks and behaviors. And it needs a
new slogan—nothing could be more off the mark than
this one. If slogans just seem like inconsequential words
to you, think again. Words are power tools.

❏   Words in this World   ❏

The thicket of social influences can be quite intricate,
but it's characterized by simple, often blunt words, as
shown in Table 3.1.

A short list, to be sure, but when you look over these
words, two aspects seem to jump out. Notice that for
both positive and negative words alike: (1) How many involve publicity of either the action or its consequences;
and (2) How many also result in group action or attitude
toward an individual. For now, I'll call these: (1) visibility, and (2) accountability. We can draw some basic conclusions from this, and simplify our exploration of the
thicket—then we can navigate through it.

Table 3.1   GroupThink Words

Negative Words	Positive Words
Shun	Celebrate
Embarrass	Honor
Punish	Congratulate
Ignore	Emulate
Prohibit	Encourage
Deny	Allow
Reprove	Approve
Disrespect	Esteem
Scorn	Praise
Disgust	Applause
Isolate	Invite
Reject	Welcome
Discourage	Inspire
Depress	Uplift
Taboo	Cherish

Visibility: The Light of Public Opinion

Take a quick glance at the word list again and you'll probably also notice an underlying metaphor of light versus darkness. When a person is *shunned*, he or she is cast out into the darkness—into the periphery of society—and when they're *celebrated*, the spotlight is put on them. When an act or person is an *embarrassment*, we put it out of our minds, turn away not wanting to see it (darkness). On the other hand, when we *honor* a person or action, we enjoy thinking and talking about it (light). *Ignoring* a person casts them out of our thoughts (into the darkness of our consciousness), while *emulating* them puts them in the forefront of our thinking (they serve as our beacon of light). The pattern holds with the rest, like *scorn* = dark, *praise* = light. *Reject* = you're tossed out into the darkness, *welcome* = we keep the porch light on for you. Things are looking dark (*depression*); the warm glow of public opinion (*praise*).

Only criminals are compelled by darkness.

You can't help but draw this conclusion: Good things happen in the light, they're visible, there for all to see. Conversely, bad things happen in the dark; we'd just as soon not see them at all. Isn't it true that most sins, crimes, and vices tend to take place under cover of darkness or secrecy? And isn't it also true that great acts—actions we esteem or praise happen, more often than not, out in the open? This isn't a coincidence. We're programmed this way.

Except for a few misfits, we all run away from what

"Never greet a stranger in the night, for he may be a demon."
—*The Talmud*

131

we consider bad (flee the dark) and towards what we consider good (run for the safety of the light). Saints and sinners, criminals and the law abiding, know this quite well. If you want to do something against society's norms, best to do it in the shadows, undetected. If you choose to do something society honors, it's generally done in full public view. (A wonderful exploration of this phenomenon in pre-industrial society is contained in A. Roger Ekrich's fascinating book, *At Day's Close*[4]). This is a fundamental law of the social fabric—the thicket we're exploring. Why is this pertinent? If you're a compelling person, you pull desired behavior into the light with you, and push unacceptable behavior out into the darkness.

❑ Our Darkest Fears ❑

All business leaders everywhere, in every industry, share one mutual fear: They're afraid something bad is happening "out there" or "down there" among their employees, customers, competitors. Something is going on that they don't know about. Something threatening is brewing, and could jump out and bite them right in their market share or cash flow. They absolutely hate the specter of a shocking surprise like this. They spend millions on information systems to keep tabs on the details of their operations (what they do), and they spend more millions on business intelligence, marketing studies, and the like (what the others are doing). You can't blame them.

Ignorance is not bliss. It's fear.

Responsible parents have similar dreads. What's our son doing out with those guys? What happens when we leave our teenage daughter at home for a weekend alone? Is she really going to the library, or somewhere we don't know about? Just who is this new boyfriend, anyway? What's he doing on the internet so long every night? More fear of the dark. And you can't blame them.

Then there are politicians, who always have their nose to the prevailing winds. What are the voters thinking? What's my opponent up to? What heat will I face in the election if I vote for this bill? What are the hot buttons I can push in this speech? What group will I offend if I take this stand? And you can't blame them, either. (Well, you can—but not for this human trait.)

Of course, some universal fears make everyone's list: Is this just a stomach ache, or cancer? Does he/she really love me? Will I ever be able to retire? What does my future hold? What happens when I die? More unknowns, more fear, more darkness.

Millions of Children Disappear—Overnight

Since the mid 1970s the U.S. Internal Revenue Service (IRS) has been doing something most American's aren't aware of and would hardly expect. We know this agency as tax collectors, the government arm that takes money from citizens. *But they also give money away*, and a whole lot of it. This is their Earned Income Tax Credit program (EITC). The intention is to stimulate a work ethic among those living on the bottom rung of the economic ladder—to promote work over welfare. To ease the tax burden on these folks and encourage them to be wage earners, the EITC allows for heads of household (sole support of children under the age of 18) who earned wages below a certain level to get a tax credit (not a deduction, but an actual gift of several thousand dollars each tax year).

Word got out, and many deserving families were assisted this way. But over time, fraud reared its ugly head. People without children were claiming they had them to qualify for the money. Cottage industries of shady "counselors" aided in this deception, helping the unqualified fill out the forms and pose as qualified. So in 1987 the ever-so-alert IRS took the new step of requiring each applicant to list not only the names but the Social Security numbers of each child claimed. As soon as the child was born, parents were asked to register him or her in the Social Security System and receive a unique identification number—just as if they were grown-ups working on a job. This didn't have a thing to do with Social Security eligibility or those benefits—it was just a way of tracking the identity and existence of children claimed under the dependent provisions of the income tax laws. This was well-publicized and an outreach effort made sure everyone knew about it in advance. But when the effective filing year came around, something strange and unexpected happened.

Want to change behavior? Shine light where darkness prevailed.

Seven million American children, "representing about one in ten of all dependent children in the United States," disappeared overnight.[5] They simply vanished into thin air. Kids who were listed on last year's returns were simply no more. And surprise, no mass graves were ever found. Heaven must've been very crowded.

Billions of tax dollars were saved, simply by shining a little light on this scam. Since then, the IRS has implemented even more active validation efforts, but still estimates say that as much as $10 billion a year is currently lost through fraud and error in this one program. Imagine how much worse it would be if all those kids hadn't suddenly decided to turn into phantoms?

This isn't foreign to us. We've all walked into a dark

kitchen for a midnight snack, turned on the lights, and watched cockroaches scurry away. Bad stuff doesn't like the spotlight.

❑ The Power of Visibility ❑

Want to know the quickest, most powerful method of getting people to lose weight? It isn't a drug or even a new exercise machine. It's not hypnosis, and it isn't a doctor's warning. It's a high school reunion. These happen every ten years or so, and in the months preceding them pounds start to melt away. Diets work, exercise suddenly gets serious. Sure, there are some who really don't care how they appear to former classmates and don't get caught up in this drill. But they are few and far between (most of them are naturally slender anyway). The vast majority of us care deeply about how we're viewed by our peers; we highly value, and fear, their judgment of us.

We want the good words attached to us (*honor, respect, emulate, praise, applause*) and we fear the bad ones (*embarrass, disrespect, shun, scorn*).

That's because a lot of us live in relative obscurity during the years between these reunions. We're in different areas of the world, working and living with those who have no memory of our youthful days and our younger appearance. They have no basis against which to compare how we look. But our old friends certainly do. They're sure to compare you to their mental models of you 10, 20, or more years ago. *Compare* is an important term here—comparing what we look like to what we used to look like. The power of visibility relies on these comparisons.

To continuously compel others, especially when the transition is rough and long, use comparisons as much as you can. Compare what's been achieved to what was planned. Compare what was expected to what was encountered. Like with the digital watch on the marathoner, these comparisons always help. If they're behind schedule, or missing expectations, visibility into this difference encourages a redoubling of efforts (We're slower than we thought, better speed up.) And if they're ahead, progressing better than expected, visibility into this condition maintains momentum and spurs even further improvement. (We're hitting all the right targets, better keep it up). Either way, visibility works.

> **People can't improve unless they know precisely *what* and *how* to improve.**

Public notice of private effort is a boon to improvement. Public ignorance of private effort is its bane. Compelling people spotlight the good and the bad. Bad improves and good gets better. As long as this is done regularly, and with respect rather than humiliation, it powers individuals and groups over difficult challenges and into different futures—what compelling is all about.

This starts early in life, and continues to the very end. Our first school report card is a visible record of accomplishments and failures. Getting good grades? Keep it up, what you're doing is to be celebrated and continued. Getting low grades? Let's work on this, see if we can improve next round. Teachers know this power and can vouch for it. As soon as a disturbing report card is carried home, parents who haven't given school a second thought suddenly become interested and energized. A report card is, in a real sense, like a mini-reunion. It shines light on what has previously been undetected or underappreciated. And it's another comparison: What we did last term vs. what we did this term. What we were expected to do vs. what we did. What we should know vs. what we do know.

Same thing with an annual physical at the doctor's office. Here's what you should weigh, and here's how you actually tipped the scales. Here's the safe range for blood pressure, and here's how yours compares. Here's the amount of a certain chemical in your blood vs. the normal range. If everything falls within acceptable ranges, you walk away satisfied and determined to maintain your level of health—to avoid the temptations that would detract from it. If not, if an "out-of-range" condition is found, you and the doctor devise ways to rectify it. Normal or abnormal, good results or troubling ones, this visibility helps. Again, ignorance isn't bliss—it's fear.

Companies reengineering their processes (trying to improve) use this extensively. They employ proven programs called "continuous improvement," "quality circles," and "Six Sigma" doctrines to aggressively plan, measure, compare, and readjust accordingly. Hospitals, factories, call centers, help desks, universities—you name it, this principle applies across the board. These big, expensive programs are no different from the high school reunion, report card, or doctor's visit. They all involve feedback, positive or negative, to compel us to either change or keep on changing. Feedback loops are at the heart of *control theory*. If we're really interested in affecting and sustaining outcomes, we should look at this more closely.

❑ Quick Look at Control Theory ❑

Its roots go back to WWII, when gunners needed to track targets. Missing to the right? Aim more to the left. Missing low? Aim higher. Measure how you did, adjust what you do next. That's about it—pretty simple. Of course, control theory grew, got much more complex. It evolved into a separate science, with its own brand of mathematics, and it helped usher in the computer age. All this began with a simple need: People want to hit what they aim at. In that regard, it hasn't changed at all; that's precisely what compelling people want to do—hit what *they* aim at. The simple diagram in Figure 3.1 makes it clear.

Start with the top bubble, "Measure." This is how you determine what you or others are doing (not how well you're doing, just *what* you're doing—how well comes next). Follow down to "Compare." Here you match what you measured against some sort of standard, like those in the box to the right. This tells you how well you're doing. In this example that standard might be your weight *goal* for the reunion, or the grade you *expect* your child to earn in school. It might be what *others* are

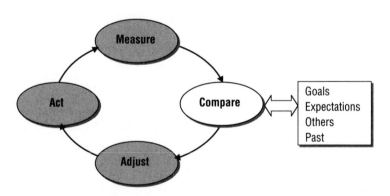

Figure 3.1   Control Theory in a Simple Diagram

doing, like when a corporate CEO uses "benchmarking" against his competitors. And it could be what's been done in the *past* (like how much you weighed in high school, or how well you did on last term's report card for a particular subject). Regardless of the standard you use (and remember, compelling people choose that standard), you can't adjust—the next step—unless you know what to adjust and by how much—that's why comparison is so crucial.

Following this comparison, the necessary changes are made (if required) and we continue to act. Then we go around the figurative circle again, and again, constantly refining what we're doing, measuring and comparing to our standard, until we achieve the outcomes we intended.

The magic in this cycle occurs on the right side of the diagram. This is where feedback loops come into play, where bad stuff gets fixed (negative feedback) and good stuff gets encouraged (positive feedback). Positive feedback says, "Keep it up, do more of this!" and negative feedback says, "Whoa, this isn't working. Stop doing it!" Compelling people are masters at both loops.

Closed-loop systems are all over the place. We rely on them to regulate our home heating and air conditioning. Thermostats are closed-loop devices. Too hot? Turn off the furnace. Too cold? Fire it up again. And closed-loop systems run the cruise control on our cars. Too fast? Slow down. Too slow? Speed up. They aren't just mechanical, either. Consider the grades on your child's report card. Too low? Time for more study. Too high? Maybe you should go out for the basketball team and broaden your experiences (just get a good, store-bought jock strap).

Main message: No feedback, positive or negative, occurs when you can't see what's going on and thereby compare it to what you intend. That's why visibility—frequent, specific, no-place-to-hide visibility, is so important. Turn the light on and keep it on.

❏ Accountability: The Other Weapon ❏

Suppose you do visit your doctor for that annual exam and a host of concerns arise. You walk out and tell the doctor, over your shoulder, "Yeah doc, we do have some problems." To which your doctor should reply "Hey! What's this 'we' stuff?" Laughable, maybe, but not farfetched.

If you've ever worked in any kind of organization, you've lived this. The boss calls a staff meeting on a pressing issue. Everyone shows up, sits around a table, takes notes and talks about how bad things are. Charts plot the details on a white board or projection screen. Opinions are aired, possible remedies floated. Everyone agrees: "We" have an issue here. Then time runs out, everyone gathers up their stuff and hits the door. Nothing changes. Responsibility for a solution vanishes, gets sucked up by some invisible ether.

Hospital staff convene a meeting. Hospital-induced infections are on the rise. We must address this. Doctors, nurses, administrators fret and debate the causes. Everyone agrees: "We" need to fix this. Then the shift is over, the white coats rush out into the hallway, and nothing happens. It's got to be that ether again.

The team is losing and the coach gathers players in the locker room at half-time. "We're behind by 14 points," he laments. "We need to start playing like a team, not a bunch of self-interested individuals." All heads nod. They run back onto the playing field, each convinced that "We" need to take our game to a higher level. Problem is, "We" isn't in the lineup, he's not on the roster. What position does "We" play, anyhow? Answer: "We" doesn't exist. *"We" is the ether that sucks up individual responsibility.*

"We" isn't accountable for anything.

In almost all organizations, particularly large ones, personal accountability is often lost in the mechanics of action or buried deep within the strata of the organization itself. "The culture of the organization runs strongly to the shifting of problems to others—to an escape from personal mental effort and responsibility."[6] Do everything possible to prevent this escape.

Side note: This is the fourth time we've seen the term "escape" used here:

1. Escape from the *Complex*—our human predilection for simplicity and immediacy.
2. Escape from *Freedom*—how compelling people winnow many choices down to one dream.
3. Escape from *Risk*—Cortez burned his ships to prevent a return to the safe and known past.
4. Escape from *Duty*—the avoidance of personal responsibility in a group setting.

While the first three can be tools for compelling leaders, the last one is your enemy.

"We" Doesn't Exist and Never Should

At this writing the largest automobile manufacturer on earth is teetering on the edge of bankruptcy. Sales are way off, cash flow is thinning out, bond ratings are heading to the cellar, new models are met with a yawn. With tens of thousands of employees, mammoth facilities worldwide, thousands of suppliers and dealerships, and billions of dollars at stake, this is one hell of a big "We." This is General Motors. If and when it implodes, "We" won't care a bit. "We" won't lose a dollar. Corporations don't lose money, never have.

Corporations are fictitious legal contrivances (ether). They're thoughts, not things, and they certainly aren't people. When the corporation goes belly-up investors (real people) lose money, workers (real people) lose jobs, vendors (more real people) lose contracts, and customers lose service. When a hospital infects patients, it doesn't get sick or die—individuals do. When the team wins a championship, it doesn't get to wear a ring. Only the people on the roster get this privilege. When a student receives a failing mark, the school isn't put back a grade—the student is. And, most importantly, when things need to change, "We" opts out. "We" disappears. You never compel a "We." You compel individuals, or you don't compel at all.

Groups don't win or lose. People do.

And Take Names

Every profession, team, institution, and other grouping has its own special monikers for someone they honor or emulate. In the art world, a new artist might be called a "free spirit" or a "breath of fresh air." This is a community that treasures difference, creativity—a new way of looking at things. In the commercial marketplace, a top sales representative is called a "rainmaker," someone who makes things happen. A well-read, interested-in-everything academic is a "Renaissance man" among his peers. A big-time gambler is a "player" or a "high roller."

An all-star professional athlete is a "franchise maker." All are honorifics peculiar to a specific subculture of like-minded individuals. Sought-after labels in subdivisions of the social thicket.

Want it done? Attach a name to it.

Inducted into the Army, I ran into such an honorific my first day. "I'm Sergeant Johnson," he yelled to my group of newly-drafted soldiers fresh off the bus. "And I kick ass and take names!" Despite having only a ninth grade education, Sgt. Johnson had cracked the code of accountability that often baffles CEOs and other would-be leaders. In his subculture, kicking ass and taking names meant something, it was quite an honorific—a sought-after label (it's no coincidence that the First Sergeant of every Army company is called the "top kick"). It meant that if you fouled up, in addition to being criticized or punished, you would be held personally accountable for what you did or didn't do. Your name would be taken. Not the name of your Army unit (your squad, platoon, or company), but *your* name. Nothing is more personal than your name. Accountability begins here—with names.

Compelling people tie actions and consequences, good or bad, to individuals by name. Only individuals are accountable. And this is as it should be, for only individuals change. You never compel "them," you compel each and every one of "them." The collective result may be a change in the group, but responsibility and accountability aren't group attributes, they're individual duties.

Postscript: Not only did Sgt. Johnson know the magic of accountability, he also practiced a lesson we covered earlier in the *Message* chapter. His message was logical enough. Do well, no problem. Do poorly, you get punished and your name remembered (left brain). We stood and listened intensely, looking at this imposing authority figure standing proudly there in his spit-shined, gleaming boots. The standard shoe polish the Army used then was Kiwi brand, and Sgt. Johnson must've used a lot on those boots. Then he added an amendment. "If you don't do exactly what I tell you, when I tell you, I'm going to put my boot so far up your ass your breath will smell like Kiwi!" Bang—a direct hit in the right brain. Our intellects *and* our emotions were magnetized to his cause.

❏ **Examples** ❏

Situation One: You're Vice President of Sales for a national retail chain. Your hundreds of stores are divided into four regions: Northeast, South, Midwest, and West. Sales have been down for several months and you call a meeting of regional sales leaders.

147

Generalities aren't actionable. Specifics are.

Bad example: "I will not stand for one more month of falling sales," you tell them. "We're running behind by six million this quarter alone." You show a large bar chart that demonstrates this continuous decline. There, for all to see, is a line showing budgeted amounts for the entire chain, by month, against actual sales figures. It isn't pretty. "You guys are looking like a bunch of losers. I expect November's numbers to beat quota by at least 5 percent, and I will hold all of you responsible if we miss this!"

Okay, you've used control theory and feedback loops. You've measured sales and compared them against a standard (your annual target budget). Now everyone knows the exact deficit that exists, and you've given them a new, specific target in the short term. So far, so good. But then you fall down on the job of leadership. Sgt. Johnson would not be pleased. You haven't insisted on accountability. Regions may put up good or bad numbers each month, but regions ("We") don't make sales. You've smeared accountability across the entire sales force, spread it very thin over everyone, as a group. Net effect: Very little will change. The top sales people will mentally check out, they know this doesn't apply to them. After all, they're above quota. This is someone else's problem. And the poor performers in the group, the ones who should own the problem and the solution, look from right to left sheepishly—and keep quiet. They're off the hook. This is a company problem, and surely the company will solve it. Or will they?

Good example: You show the first sales chart to get their attention; yes, we do have a company issue here. But then you show a second chart that breaks the national numbers down into regional ones, and further, into a store-by-store comparison of plan vs. actual sales for each specific store that has failed to meet their targets. "These seven stores," you conclude, "are causing most of our trouble. Reed," you say, pointing her out in the crowd, "you're in charge of the South, and you've got five of these stores: # 2304, 2387, 2409, 2776 and 2876. Go to Richmond and Raleigh next week, and, by Friday, tell me what needs to be done to fix this." Then you point to a second sales manager. "Rodriguez, you've got stores #3433 and 3567. You come to me on Friday after you've been to Los Angeles and San Diego. I want the same answer."

Before they leave, you make one final point. "Hollins and Dandridge have consistently outperformed in their regions. I want you both to help out here. So Hollins, you go with Reed and report back with her. Dandridge, you accompany Rodriguez out west. Help your counterpart determine what is causing this and what must be done to fix it." Note the use of names, dates, specific actions. The stuff of accountability. Sgt. Johnson would be smiling.

Situation Two: Your software development company is bidding on a big job for a new client. You've assigned the RFP (Request for Proposal) to a team of a dozen people, who've been working feverishly on the proposal, against a tight deadline. After struggling for days, unable to come up with a concept and design that would meet your price estimates, team member Deborah Clemens remembers a previous proposal she worked on a few years ago. The client and application were different, but the basics were very similar. She suggests using it as a template, adapting some of its design and cost estimates. This works—the proposal is finished quickly, submitted, and chosen by the client. You won the engagement, and bring in a keg of beer Friday afternoon so the team can celebrate their victory.

Every leader holds a figurative GroupThink gun in his or her hands. It has a dial with many settings—positive and negative. You're happy, and want to turn the dial on your GroupThink gun to "good job."

Bad example: "I'm here to congratulate this team on a superb job," you announce, holding up a cup of brew. "You came up with an innovative solution and an excellent design. Great proposal! Let's give you all the credit you deserve!" Everyone hoists their drinks and gives a group cheer.

Problem: The group didn't come up with the design or concept—Deborah Clemens did. Some group members contributed absolutely nothing, except maybe confusion and resistance. The outcome of group effort might be successful, but, in this case, the cause of that success is an individual. Just as individuals must be held accountable for bad results, individuals must be praised when good ones occur. The slackers in this group are getting the same kudos as the real champion, who prevailed despite their obstruction. I forgot to mention this earlier: Sgt. Johnson not only kicked slacker ass, he also dispensed coveted three-day passes. Ms. Clemens deserves one.

Good example: "We won," you tell the group. "And we won despite the fact that this is a client and industry we knew very little about. I don't know how we'd have gotten this job without the insight and effort of Deborah Clemens." A round of applause erupts, directed towards Deborah. "We give away bonuses from time to time, for people who go above and beyond the call of duty. Deborah, would you please come over and accept our gratitude and this check?"

Maybe it's not a check, maybe your company doesn't provide this type of incentive. But for heaven's sake, call out Deborah for special praise—public praise. She lives in this company thicket and surely appreciates some good words attached to her, by name. Words like *honor,* *congratulate, esteem* and *applause.* And you might want to follow up with her and find out who really contributed and who, if anyone, gummed things up. They say success has many parents and failure is an orphan. Some of those success parents may be hangers on—ones who just cruise along for the ride while others do the real work. Don't let this persist for long. Even when groups win, individuals within them aren't equally responsible for victory.

Another point here: Notice you give her the check right there, on the spot, in front of her peers. This is a fundamental lesson in leadership. Praise and punishment should swiftly follow the activity that earns either. Don't let Deborah get her check in the mail a few months from now, under cover of darkness. Shine the good light brightly and quickly.

> **Praise and punishment should be swift and sure.**

❏ **Escape from Anonymity** ❏

This entire I-them, me-us dichotomy is a recurring theme here. *Like us, unlike us* keeps reappearing. Some may call me to task on this, pointing out that different cultures see the individual-group relationship in a different way. I learned this in Japan, a society that places a different emphasis on the question. Cultural norms are strong, group identity is highly valued in Japan. They have a wonderful expression, which translates to "the nail that stands out gets the hammer." Against this backdrop, inside this thicket, I was asked to teach *innovation*—standing out from the crowd—thinking and acting differently. I flew to Tokyo bracing myself for the hammer.

I like to teach through activity, using exercises interspersed with the lecture format—a hands-on experience is much more helpful than a dry recitation of rules. So I typically design these into the program of learning. I'll take a room full of participants and divide them into teams, usually those sitting at the same table. When the time comes to explore execution issues—how one applies what I've been espousing—I'll ask each table to nominate a spokesperson, review the exercise, maybe complete a worksheet, then have him or her present the table's findings and recommendations, in turn with the other tables, to the class as a whole. Pretty standard stuff for trainers. Or so I thought.

This group in Tokyo was made up of middle-aged Japanese executives, men (all men) who'd been around and had a lot of gray hair to prove it. The average age, in my estimation, was 55 or 60 years. An hour into the session, the time had come for the first exercise. Okay, I told them (thank goodness they all understood English), now we'll turn to the first exercise. I'm passing out the worksheets. Each table represents a group, so you'll first nominate a group leader. Once you've finished, I'll ask each group leader to stand up in front of the class and present your findings and recommendations. I was met with blank stares. Maybe I said it wrong? Maybe they didn't understand me? Expecting them to start discussing this among each other, I was surprised to see nothing of the sort. They sat silently, as if waiting further instruction. I repeated this, and still, nothing happened. Nobody moved or spoke. Anxious enough to begin with, I was really sweating now.

> **This tension between the individual and the group exists everywhere, at every time.**

Then my host stepped in for the rescue. "They don't work this way," he whispered in my ear. "You must appoint a leader for each table." Hmmm. Then I walked around the classroom pointing at each table in turn. "Table 1," I said, "Satoh-san is the leader. Table 2, Takahashi-san is the leader" and on through the rest of the tables. A collective sigh of relief ensued. As each table's leader was nominated, that table began to feverishly apply itself to the task at hand. Problem solved. Afterwards my host explained: Japanese feel uncomfortable electing or selecting an individual to represent the group. This is rude to suggest, and, for those selected, uncivil to accept.

By nominating a person to be in charge, I removed this social stigma. I eliminated the need for these gentlemen to be "the nail that stands out."

This story doesn't dampen my enthusiasm for individual responsibility and accountability. It strengthens it. After all, when a company goes under, or a scandal is revealed, the Japanese leaders take the bullet—they voluntarily resign, admitting fault. I deeply admire this. The question here isn't how a group chooses a leader, it's how that leader acts. These Japanese gentlemen acted as we all want our leaders, and followers, to act. It was just a question of how they are chosen. All the rules we've covered still apply. Adapt them as you will, but they still stand. We are all human, and we all share this set of questions: Who am I? and How do I fit in with my world? We just address them a bit differently. But the tension between me-them, like us and unlike us, still holds.

Individuals deserve honorifics like "top kick" and "rainmaker," but leaders who are understandably proud of their groups tend to give out collective praise as well. I've heard quite a few of these. The partner-in-charge of a large accounting firm once told me "My people move mountains!" The head of a software company once beamed "Our folks can overcome anything. They can climb out of tar pits." All very nice. But when you compel groups of individuals to a new cause, when you motivate them for big change, they won't be moving mountains or climbing out of tar pits. They'll be following you over a steep cliff, into a valley of darkness. This I can promise: When they follow you to the land of the new, they will suffer before they succeed. Things will get much worse before they get any better. There is but one, and only one, exception to this rule.

❏ Over the Cliff and into the Valley We Go ❏

The exception is this: When you're beating your head against a wall—not figuratively, but really knocking your skull into the bricks—as soon as you stop, things get instantly better. The glib line is "I do this only because it feels so good when I stop." This is another way of saying "Things are so bad, even down looks up to me." Maybe prisoners on Death Row fall into this category, but the rest of us, despite our problems, live in a fairly tolerable world. Compelling people aim to change this—to pull others out of their comfort zone into a new way of thinking and acting. Excepting this absurd example, every change you make in what you do and how you do it, as an individual or group, requires you to go down before you go up. To lose before you win. To fail before you succeed. This is why idealists have trouble leading—they're not expecting the hits coming their way. And it also explains why the pragmatic among us take charge when real change is necessary.

Getting others to think and act differently means upsetting the status quo—throwing their mental maps, their models of what works, into jeopardy. It means getting them to try the untested to achieved unproven results. When you mess with their earned equilibrium, their comfort in knowing who they are and how they fit into their world, you invite discomfort at the least and violent resistance at the most. Small changes or simple adjustments don't provoke this, and neither do they require compelling leaders. But real change, significant difference, surely does. You are entering a world of high-stake chances and high-impact choices. It involves the tension between challenge and contentment, achieving and enjoying, getting and having, and the biggest struggle of all: becoming and being.

Compelling people never deny difficulties ahead. They expect them and prepare to overcome them.

This journey carries risk, no doubt. And yes, if you face risk, something bad *may* happen. But if you run from it, something good *will never* happen.

No one is compelled to fail, or to lose what they have, without gaining what they want in the process. Compelling is the practice of conceiving and executing improvement in an individual or group. That's how something good happens. Problem is, something bad happens along the way—along the *change curve* (see Figure 3.2).

This is the path towards thinking and acting differently. I've drawn it on whiteboards, projected it on slides and screens, and tested it before tough audiences on six continents. Once its aspects are described, no one has ever disputed it. There is an ancient principle of scientific inquiry called *Occam's Razor* that tells us whenever there are a number of explanations for any complex phenomena, we should always choose the simplest among them. This curve is as simple, and as universal, as it gets.

The curve works this way: Imagine the dimension of time running from the past, on the left, to the future, on the right. Also imagine that improvement is upward, and deterioration, failure, or just bad things happening, is

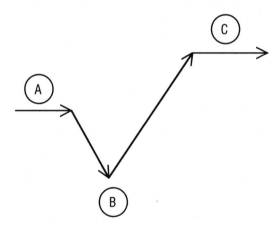

Figure 3.2   The Change Curve

down. You start at point A and, over time, you want to achieve point C (a higher level of performance, existence, or just good things happening). The principle is this: You can't jump from A to C without first going through B. You must go down before you go up. Things will get worse before they get better.

Want to lose weight? You'll have to live through Point B on the curve. You'll no doubt experience hunger pangs, have to shift to blander tasting food, skip snacks, and shell out money for new clothes before you reach your goal. Want to quit smoking? Be prepared for Point B: the pain of withdrawal, possible weight gain, increased nervousness, and patience-testing periods without tobacco. Great new job offer in a new city? Get ready for some trying times at Point B: the hassle of finding a new home, trying to sell the old one, losing friends, and distancing yourself from relatives.

Think of your own experiences shifting from what you are, or have, to what you wish to be, or want. All involve this cycle of happenings. It is undeniable, a period of uncomfortable experiences and awkward activity that is invariably upsetting and risky. But as the old saying goes, if this was easy, everyone would do it. The courage and stamina required to transverse Point B is the filter that separates those who move to the next level from those who are left behind. To be compelling, you've first got to recognize this and steel yourself for the challenge of Point B. Then learn to coax, prod, encourage, shame, and attract others along the curve. Table 3.2 gives a few examples of situations along the change curve.

Personal examples of this principle are endless. Toilet-training a child, learning a new language, breaking up a romantic relationship, changing your university major, moving to a new apartment. (You can always tell when an author has young children or grandchildren—they keep bringing up these toilet-training references. Either that, or at the end of a hard day at it, they walk into a bar and order a "Scotch and wa-wa.")

I once had a woman in the audience jump to her feet during this discussion and exclaim: "That's me and my ex-husband's divorce! On the left, at Point A, we were used to things, had a comfortable home and mutual friends, but *hated* each other. Then we had to fool with lawyers, accountants, realtors! We fought viciously over alimony and child custody! What a mess—we went through a year of absolute hell (another term for Point B). Now it's three years later, I've got a great new home, a wonderful, loving new husband, and my Ex is out of sight and out of mind. Last I heard he was off in Australia chasing sheep!" (Point C comes in many varieties).

Now extend this concept to group change. A company with a time-worn product wishing to update it to a new version has to discontinue production, shift resources, come up with a new product image, explain away the discontinued line to irritated customers, retrain sales reps, renegotiate delivery contracts, and on and on.

Table 3.2   Points along the Change Curve

Point A	Point B	Point C
A workable yet old, outdated kitchen.	Selecting contractors, spending money, enduring the construction mess, rearranging your utensils, and reordering your work habits.	A new, modern kitchen. Increased resale value for your house. A wonderful place to entertain guests.
A comfortable but go-nowhere job.	Taking admittance tests, borrowing tuition money, commuting to campus, giving up free time, studying, doing homework, listening to boring professors.	A college degree and better chance at higher-paying, more fulfilling employment.
A functional but low-tech home computer system.	Spending on new equipment, hooking up new peripherals, buying new software and learning how to use it. Saving your documents and programs and transferring them to the new devices. Tolerating the inevitable glitches and compatibility issues.	A state-of-the-art system that lets you enjoy all the features and benefits you want.
A pleasant but high-handicap golf game.	Unlearning old swings, grips, approaches. Buying new equipment. Paying for lessons. Many bad rounds as you struggle with all this to remaster the game.	An improved game and lower scores.
An employee you know well, yet who is frequently absent, unreliable, and careless.	The awkwardness of confrontation. The drama of termination. The expense of severance pay. Finding how to get the work done during the intervening period. The difficulty of interviewing and selecting a replacement. The uncertainty of how he or she will work out.	A more capable, caring, employee. Better production and fewer personal problems.

Or two companies that agree to merge. They must reconfigure their work force, often laying off hundreds of loyal but now redundant employees, combine sales territories, change their name and branding campaigns, reassure nervous customers, shift production capacity, and hundreds of other challenges during their journey from Point A (two successful, independent companies) to Point C (one integrated, competitive giant). And while they're struggling through Point B, they'll no doubt lose good employees who don't want to make the transition. They may lose customers who fear they'll be forgotten by the much larger conglomerate. And competitors will swoop down on their markets at this time of weakness, trying to steal customers and lure away key managerial and technical talent in the process. (Incidentally, validated statistics show as many as 75 percent of merged companies fail at the time of execution, what's called *post-merger integration*.)

Companies face the same change risks as individuals do. And make the same mistakes.

Commuters dissatisfied with traffic complain that something should be done to alleviate the stop-and-go, bumper-to-bumper jam-ups. They are tired of Point A (congestion, accidents, delays) and yearn for Point C (smoother traffic flow, increased speeds, safer intersections). But during the intervening months they'll face construction delays, higher taxes, detours, mud, noise, and those hideous orange traffic barrels everywhere they look. All point B stuff—irritating, aggravating, messy, and uncomfortable.

Given all these perils and problems, one has to wonder why people ever try to improve at all? If it ain't broke, wags tell us, why fix it? Why go through all this uncertainty and hardship when existing conditions, though not ideal, are at least livable? Seems like logic would suggest otherwise—that given the alternative of either staying the same or plunging over the cliff of uncertainty and into the valley of despair most people and groups would choose the former, and keep things as they are. That's true, they do.

To become compelling, you'll need the strength to pull others out of their ruts.

Individuals and companies stay in ruts, shy away from big risks. Many can't give up the known and comfortable to face the unknown and arduous. And so, in Thoreau's words, "The mass of men lead lives of quiet desperation."[7] And they will continue to do so unless some compelling person pulls them across the change curve. These special men and women may be inspired, as I am, by the writing of Kahlil Gibran, "I would rather that I died in yearning and longing than that I lived weary and despairing."[8] I never asked her, but I'm sure the woman who made it through her messy divorce, from her current vantage of Point C, would agree.

Leading, like changing, isn't so easy that anyone can do it. It requires special skills and perspectives to overcome static inertia, to plunge over the cliff. And it requires continued stamina and strength to pull others along with you, through all the Point Bs on your way to a better, more effective and enjoyable future. Compelling isn't just telling others about Point C, that shining city on a hill off in the future. It's about getting them over to it. You can teach and tantalize others all you want, but if you can't get them to follow you across this gap that separates what is from what could be, you're little more than an inconsequential tease. Yes, you will be met with resistance, and we should address this now, before moving on to ways this simple change curve will keep you from being deceived and weakened.

❑ Conquering Resistance ❑

Resistance to anything new is bound to happen, so expect and prepare for it. There are three general types of resistance:

1. **Active**—The in-your-face, defiant type.

   A few suggestions: First, find them early and deal with them quickly. Don't let their doubt and criticism drain your power and attention, or worse, infect the rest of the crowd. Another technique is to enroll them in the campaign—giving them prominent roles in the conversion from old to new. People not involved can easily act like hecklers in the seats of a sports stadium. They can jeer and taunt all day, as long as you allow them to *spectate* and not *participate*. Put them in uniform and on the field, see if they don't change their tune. If they continue to push back, set the dial on your GroupThink gun to *isolate*, *scorn*, and then *shun*. Failing these, go for the *punish* setting. You can skip the *ignore* option—this doesn't work on them.

The GroupThink gun has many settings. Don't hesitate to use the ones that work.

---

2. **Passive-Aggressive**—The ones who nod in agreement, then work behind the scenes to damage your cause.

   Or they drag their feet, gumming up your plans. Since these types seldom declare their buy-in or opposition openly, they can still be converted. This is because they don't have a public position to defend, so switching doesn't require them to explain or apologize to others. But if you ignore them, they can stab you in the back, under cover of darkness. Shine the light on this type. Give them definite roles with specific, measurable expectations—milestones to meet, deliverables to produce—real things like that (plans to produce, not *planning*). Continuously check and measure them against these standards—and do this publicly. Don't let them hide in the thicket or float along anonymously, and *never* allow them to remain noncommittal. These types need to be "outed." Setting on GroupThink gun: *accountability/visibility*—both at full strength. Setting you should never select: *ignore*.

3. **The Speed Bumps**—They just don't get it or don't care, and some never will.

Consider the persistently ignorant or apathetic as if they were living speed bumps on your road to success, and drive around or over them. Don't pay them excessive attention or worry about converting them. It's seldom worth the trouble. A lot of leadership capital can be wasted trying to get that last lost sheep into the flock. Remember, becoming compelling is about affecting outcomes, not about making everyone happy or earning their respect. For best results, set the dial on your GroupThink gun to *ignore, iso-*

late, or *reject*—your choice. Then keep driving, as if nothing happened. As you cruise towards successful outcomes, you may hear a slight thud coming from your tires, but pay it no mind. Don't even look back in your rear-view mirror at these types.

If you want to be accepted by everyone, think and do nothing new.

Another key point: Resistance doesn't just spring up when a change or new idea is announced. Quite often it hides, festering and gaining virulence as your effort unfolds. This because it's easy to go along with a new program at the very beginning, when it's not much more than an idea, a possibility. But once it starts to take shape, once real changes begin—and real pain and inertia are felt (approaching Point B)—that's when resistance either creeps silently or leaps unexpectedly into the picture. So keep alert to it during all phases of any change you're putting across: beginning, middle, and end.

Resistance is loyalty to the past and present. You must shift their loyalty to the future.

❑ The Staggered Experience Curve ❑

The division manager called me into his office and I could tell he was exasperated. He sat down, threw his hands up in surrender mode, and sighed. "They just don't get it!" His company was in the midst of a massive reorganization, a very necessary and carefully considered one. Three months into this, his people were still complaining and resisting. "Why is it?" he demanded, "Why is it that I'm the only one who sees the benefit of this?" His frustration was understandable, and extremely common among executives trying to institute a new order of things. He was absolutely correct—he was, in fact, the only one who saw the benefit of this. He was facing the *staggered experience curve* and didn't know it. He should have seen it coming.

Compelling people see the future before others and get to it much quicker. That's because they get a head start. They spend time analyzing problems, evaluating alternative solutions, crafting a dream, and justifying it to their colleagues and superiors. Then, once all this is done, they present it to the unsuspecting crowd and expect instant acceptance and swift execution. But the world simply doesn't work that way. The people in his division are going through the same anguish, the same confrontation with the new, that he did months ago. They're a few steps behind in the journey, and they're experiencing entirely different circumstances. That's why "they just don't get it." Take a look at Figure 3.3.

168

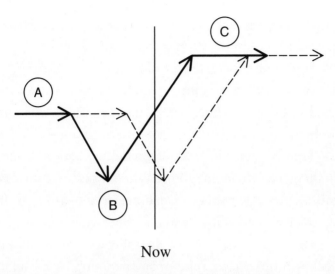

Now

Figure 3.3   The Staggered Experience Curve

The solid line is our change curve, the one the boss is traveling on. The dashed counterpart is the same curve, just shifted to the right, to the future a few months, and it represents the journey employees are experiencing. At present (time "Now") the boss has mentally traveled through Point B, accepted the hits, and is climbing upward to the goal—he can see it now, it's within reach. He's getting a sniff of improved sales, lower costs, streamlined processes, thrilled stockholders. But his people, moving along the dashed line, aren't that far along the path yet. They didn't get a head start. While he's climbing up, seeing improvement, they're still sliding down to the pits—feeling nothing but pain and discomfort.

They're getting new supervisors, strange colleagues, unfamiliar job requirements, disrupted work routines.

He's at one stage, they're at a previous one. He's "getting it" and they're getting something else. He's feeling good. They're feeling bad. That persistent *alignment* problem strikes again.

This is a classic "out of phase" condition, another challenge for the compelling. When it occurs, as it surely will, there's no reason to get upset or act surprised. It is completely predictable, and *does not* signal a problem. It signals progress. After all, if the followers were neck-and-neck with their leader, he or she wouldn't be a leader at all—just another face in the crowd. Leading means going first, experiencing choices first, making adjustments first, changing first. Give the followers the same courtesy you give yourself: time to understand and accept what's coming, time to try it out, and time to master it. They will be a bit behind you in this, and that is as it should be—and almost always is. Nothing wrong here. No reason to throw your hands up in surrender mode. This is not the time to dial the GroupThink gun to a negative setting. It's time for patience, understanding, and encouragement. They are simply not where you are. If you don't expect and prepare for this, it will be you, and not them, that doesn't "get it."

You can see this scenario in your personal lives as well. Mom is considering a transfer to a new city. It involves a bigger job title, more responsibility, a raise in pay—all that good stuff (for Mom). She considers it, weighs it against alternatives, and after a while psychologically buys into it. She may have even been to the new place, fell in love with the new job, and explored housing choices. Then she springs it on her son and daughter. They haven't done any of this. Mom's ahead of them on the experience curve, and doesn't understand why they can't accept the move. They just don't get it.

But they do get it. Problem is they're getting a different "it." They're getting a premonition of Point B all too well. The loss of friends, removal from their peer group. They're getting a foretaste of the horrors of being the new kid in town, having to start at a new high school. This bring us to a second and just as predictable problem: They're seeing a very different Point C than the one Mom's eyeing. And it's not higher than their current Point A. It's much lower. No wonder they don't buy into it.

You and *they* will *never* be on the same page—until you've finished the book.

Mom has to achieve two goals now: (1) Give them time to absorb, think through, and mentally try out this new world; and (2) Craft a more compelling, or less onerous, future for them (a Point C not as low as the one they envision). Sometimes this can be done, sometimes not. If not, Mom has to reconsider the move and make a tough decision. But she should never presume they are at the same stage of the change curve as she is, nor that her Point C is their Point C.

The staggered experience curve is a fact of life. You can't change it or wish it away. You must deal with it. As bad as this sounds, ignoring it is worse.

Corporate executives continuously stumble here. Before a change is selected, they meet and hash out the alternatives. They dry-run ways to turn their companies around, getting suggestions and input from each other. Maybe even bring in expert consultants, conduct "benchmarking" against competitors. They argue, persuade, threaten, and hold still more meetings. Finally a unilateral decision is made or a consensus achieved. No change is easy and no benefits are guaranteed, they tell themselves, but this one—the one we've devised—is our best bet. And when their employees balk at it, they're surprised. They shouldn't be. It is all part of the drill.

Know the staggered experience phenomenon and prepare for it. Use patience and understanding when you're facing an out-of-phase condition. It is simply the price we all pay for the privilege of compelling others. And yet again, it demonstrates another facet of this *like them, unlike them* conundrum we keep running across. Compelling people are *like them* in that they're riding along the same curve, but *unlike them* because they're a step or two ahead on it. For our final chapter, I would like to focus on the *unlike them* element. I want to explore ways compelling people define and display themselves. Who are they anyway?

Chapter 4

Witnessing

wit·ness·ing \ 'wit-nəs-iŋ \
1. Taking note of; observing.
2. Furnishing or servicing as evidence.

❏ Is This Seat Vacant, Madam? ❏

It was an overcast summer day in London when a black man with a slight limp was spotted pursuing a white matron into a landau on the Mall. Clutching her closely guarded purse even more tightly to her chest, she turned away as he boldly took the seat next to her. The driver, anxious to escape the milling crowds, cracked his whip and four horses pulled the carriage away. An enterprising photographer caught it all on film.

Later that same evening this unlikely pair was spotted drinking together in a posh establishment, raising and touching glasses in toast. The most unimpeachable witnesses will swear to it. Further investigation reveals the man is an ex-convict, just recently out of prison. A foreigner, he has a long history of criminal arrests. Most intriguing, his given name, "Rolihlahla," translates to "Troublemaker." Eventually, over 1,000 Londoners were questioned, with 222, exactly 19.8 percent, fingering the black man by name. He would be summoned by the House of Lords for his many acts of defiance.

Readers of mysteries will be forgiven for next expecting a messenger to arrive at 221b Baker Street, London, inquiring after Mr. Sherlock Holmes. But the carriage ride took place in 1996, not 1886. The matron was Elizabeth Alexandra Mary Windsor, Queen Elizabeth II, and her unlikely male companion—the troublemaker—was Nelson Rolihlahla Mandela, President of the Republic of South Africa (given the name Nelson by a primary schoolteacher to honor the British naval hero, Admiral Lord Nelson). The posh establishment wherein they lifted glasses together is Buckingham Palace. It was a long-awaited state visit between two very different symbols. The world witnessed it on television, which also recorded, at a later visit, the Queen bestowing on Mandela the Order of St. John. As for the man being hauled before the House of Lords, this too was a public honor. The Nobel Peace Prize winner was awarded the Queen's Council by this august group in May 2000.

But what of the fingering of this individual by questioned Londoners? This was the result of a survey taken by the Museum of London between November 2001 and May 2002. Among a list of questions, one asked "What person do you most admire?" The number-one choice was Nelson Mandela (19.8 percent). Queen Elizabeth II ranked near the bottom, earning just 3.8 percent of responses. Keep in mind, the poll was taken of visitors to the Museum of London, not inmates at Robben Island or Pollsmoor Prisons, in which Nelson Mandela spent some 27 years.

This is a chapter about symbols, emblems, brands, images, and how they're seen and heard by others. About building evidence that a new proposal is genuine and enduring, worth following through hardship and uncertainty. How compelling people personalize their cause and lead others to identify with it. In all the world, I don't believe I could come up with two more dramatically different symbols than the Queen and Mandela, two very unlikely fellow travelers in the carriage of history. We will use them as character foils, polar opposites that, when considered side-by-side, reveal the very essence of our theme.

Their similarities first. Both were born to royalty, the Queen to a long line of monarchs stretching back centuries; Mandela's father was counselor to Chiefs of the Thembu Tribe. Upon his father's death, Mandela was raised by the tribe's Regent. The Queen ascended her throne upon her father's death. She assumed reign at the age of 25. He had to wait longer, enduring years of scorn and captivity until becoming the first democratically elected president of his nation at age 76. He ruled his country for just three years. The Queen has been on the throne for more than half a century.

This last fact holds the key to their diverse mandates and reveals why each was so fitted to their individual destinies. For the Queen has one job, one duty: to keep things as they are—for a very long time. To preserve a treasured heritage handed down from generation to generation. To maintain, to guard the status quo. Mandela, on the other hand, had a different charge. His fate was to create massive social change—and quickly. To vilify an oppressive heritage, overthrow the status quo. To compel generations of others to think and act differently.

We may appreciate the Queen for dutifully meeting her obligations. This she has done, despite some embarrassing incidents among her family members. Mandela had a few of these as well. But appreciating is not the same as following. Stewards keep things as they are, leaders make things as they should be. In the contest for most admirable person, no wonder the *leader* outscored the *steward* five to one. As a whole, we have less respect for those who keep things as they are than we do for those who make them better. Control and continuity may be necessary and even arduous, but they are not compelling.

In the days immediately after Mandela's fete at Buckingham Palace, the Queen was filmed reviewing an ancient military regiment, standing at stiff attention with requisite purse clutched tightly to her side, topped by a prim hat. Mandela was filmed across town at a tree-planting ceremony, celebrating newness, growth, and dancing joyously to the beat of an African band.

Which is more memorable and inspiring? The Queen supervising her minions in the proper table setting for a dignified royal dinner, or the convict teaching philosophy and Greek drama to fellow inmates in a dank prison cell? Smuggling notes out via friends, with messages like "Any man or institution who tries to rob me of my dignity will lose."

Compelling people do not control or overpower others. They get them to think and act differently, with outcomes benefiting both parties in this struggle: the leader and the followers. They do this with symbols, events and accomplishments others respect and value. And they never rob anyone of their dignity. In fact, they think and act with *earned* dignity at all times. Compelling isn't about manipulation, deceit, or taking advantage of others. It's about finding and releasing the potential within us all to achieve improvement, even greatness. As Andre Brink, a professor at the University of Cape Town, said of Mandela, "He has reaffirmed our common potential to move toward a new age."

❏   Bang on the Symbols   ❏

Reading this story of the Queen and Nelson Mandela, you may have noticed how I liberally used symbols to create the scene and characters and to make their point. Table 4.1 lists the loaded words and phrases used.

These words and phrases are symbols—they make an instant impression by referring to contexts and values bigger than themselves. This is how an entire sequence of events and characters, played out against a rich and contrasting background, can be condensed into a few brief paragraphs. That's the power of symbols. Compelling people know how to select and use them, how to tie their cause to honored ones, and how to use dishonored or unvalued ones for the alternatives they seek to avoid (doing nothing, taking another route, choosing another leader).

Table 4.1   Symbols for Two Different Leaders

Queen Elizabeth II	*Nelson Mandela*
White matron, clutching her closely-guarded purse	Black man with a slight limp boldly took the seat next to her
Prim	Ex-convict
Stiff attention	Troublemaker
Monarchs	Foreigner
Duty, obligation	Criminal arrests
Continuity, control	Many acts of defiance
Throne	Tribal chiefs
Treasured heritage	Oppressive heritage
Dignified, royal dinner	Dank prison cell

Symbols work for a number of reasons: (1) They simplify your message and cause; (2) They appeal across organizational and cultural boundaries, and (3) They save time and effort when identifying or communicating with others.

The business executive crossing the Pacific in a jetliner wears his expensive Rolex watch to symbolize his wealth, taste, and perhaps power. He can't wave his resume around the first class compartment, flaunt his property deeds, or run a PowerPoint presentation on his assets and liabilities, his net worth. The Rolex does this for him. It's recognized wherever he travels, and, he hopes, makes an instant, favorable impression on those he meets. So it's simple, quick, informative, and universal, four characteristics of a good symbol. It's the embodiment of an unmistakable message he wishes to convey: "I am somebody." All this without opening his mouth or his briefcase (after all, that may cause him to lift his Gucci shoes off his Tumi carryon and disturb the Coach purse of the female exec sporting the Hermes scarf and snoozing next to him!).

Further back, no doubt in economy class, sits a bearded gentleman in a worn tweed jacket, complete with leather elbow patches. He is hunched over a book, reading intensely over his half-cut eyeglasses. Sporting comfortable suede shoes and sipping a glass of red wine, he glances at his black plastic wristwatch. It tells the exact time, with the same or better degree of accuracy as the aforementioned Rolex, at less than one percent of the cost. But this man has a very different image to project. He's a university professor, and looks it. His symbol set achieves the same purpose as the business leader's: I am somebody.

Across the aisle a woman fingers a rosary and sighs. She's deep into a thick book of thin, onion-skin paper. Her graying, short-cropped hair, modest dress and lack of cosmetics and jewelry tell another story. She's a nun, and she is somebody too.

These symbols are our first example of the phenomenon of witnessing, and they fit the definition at the opening of this chapter. They allow others "to take note, or observe," and they "furnish or serve as evidence" of each person's wealth, position, or devotion to a cause. Symbols, then, have two requirements to meet: They must be observable, and they must say something. If they miss the first requirement, they're just trinkets. If they miss the second test, they're just noise—irrelevant distractions. This is an important lesson: Choose and use your symbols wisely.

We all wear, drive, live in, and identify with our own symbols. Take symbols away and half of all goods and services sold in the affluent and not-so-affluent sectors of the world suddenly become meaningless. So much for the Range Rovers, Mont Blanc's, Armani's, and all the other objects that exist as much to broadcast a message as to perform a utilitarian function. Even those who scoff at convention and ridicule the status-seeking among us have their own symbols. Tattoos, green hair, baggy low-riding pants, bling-bling accoutrements, and body piercing—they proclaim individualism and an anti-establishment attitude—until you look around the airplane, airport, and city street and see hundreds of others looking almost identical. Here we find, yet again, this *like them-unlike them* dichotomy of human experience. These renegades (*unlike* them because I am a successful business exec, esteemed intellectual, or pious servant of God) are all wearing uniforms (*like* those of my type—my class, profession, or religious persuasion), and thereby rendezvousing with like-minded members of the group they've joined. They are fulfilling the requirements of their mental models. Their symbols validate this to themselves and others. They are demonstrating that, at least for now, they know the answer to our two basic philosophical questions: (1) Who am I?, and (2) How do I fit into the world?

Symbols let us show how we are *like* and *unlike* others. Treat them with respect.

When you ask others to move to a new way of thinking and acting, you're upsetting this equilibrium. You may even be trashing their cherished symbols. Be careful when you do this that you don't stir a negative, defensive response. Wresting away symbols of self and group identity from those who, like Queen Elizabeth II, clutch them tightly to their chest, is dangerous business. Always remember that, except for prisoners and slaves, most of us *chose* these symbols. Most of us have intentionally selected, accommodated, or justified the way we think and act—the way we live. And to all but a very few, our symbols *are* us. Proceed with caution.

❏ The Need for Evidence ❏

Symbols come in all shapes and sizes: corporate logos, advertising tag lines, team uniforms, flags, and military insignia. Generally simple and bold, they stand out for our attention and recognition. Many historic quests begin under the symbol of a larger entity: a nation, religion, or common cause (lust for money, fear of outsiders, righteousness of "our way"). But the real power of symbols isn't here—it's not at the beginning of a dangerous change, but in the middle of one, when things start to get rough. When doubt sets in and resolve weakens. When things go bad before we have any assurance they will eventually get better. Symbols are the embodiment of ideals and dreams, and like them, are easy to accept when the price isn't high—at the beginning of a journey. But when we approach and hit Point B, we need symbols more than ever. This is when they prove their value.

Witnessing

This is when we need evidence we're doing the right thing; we need witnesses that this is going to work. Witnesses are fellow group members who can attest to the value of the cause and the wisdom of pursuing it. Ones who are the first to spot land while crossing an ocean of uncertainty. Proof, of sorts, that we should persevere in the face of hardship. And most importantly, that this exercise is for real—it isn't a wild goose chase or a soon-to-fade fad.

> **The time to strike up the band is during the silence of despair.**

I once owned a small company that specialized in change management consulting. We were acquired by a larger firm with a more general market and broader "solution set." Just when I was getting them acquainted with what we did and slightly comfortable with how change management would bolster their bottom line, they were, in turn, bought by an even larger, more distant company. The giant firm bought them for what they traditionally did, and had no knowledge of my subspecialty. I was a kind of unknown and uninteresting quality hidden deep inside the prize they'd purchased. They didn't buy me, they bought them. I was just baggage, a tiny freebee tossed into the package.

My challenge was convincing the larger firm to keep

this capability, and, if possible, embrace its distant potential and invest further in it. They could have easily tossed it out—it was far from their core competence, and not a speck on their strategic maps. In two months, top management was to hold a strategy session to determine how the overall company, including the recent purchase, would move ahead. Tension among us "acquired" was high.

I scheduled a seminar to introduce change management to selected members of both larger firms immediately prior to the big strategic get-together. Since that meeting would be held in London, many of us would be travelling overseas. Adding two days to the front end of this trip was entirely reasonable. About 30 mid-management types from around the world agreed to attend my session. For two days the concept and market were laid out before them, and the reception was very positive.

I continued to make the case for change management at every possible opportunity, buttonholing each individual attendee during breaks, at meals, and over coffee and drinks. Would this specialty work in their districts, their countries? Could it bolster what they offered their clients? Would it be aligned with their markets? Almost all answered yes to each question. They liked it, and wanted to start building this new capability in their home markets. But they weren't the decision-makers. The big guys weren't there yet, but were presently flying in for the major meeting. And the big guys weren't sentimental or loyal to anything at this time. They had money to make.

We convened in a Hyatt hotel just outside Heathrow airport. Of the 30 managers who attended my pre-session, about seven or eight were senior enough to be invited. As for the rest—the big guys—I knew none of them. But they offered me a precious 30-minute time slot to present my case to the assembled crowd on the first day. Whether I'd be invited to continue at the meeting after that, or take an earlier flight home, was very questionable. I had a complex message and an unproven business plan, and I'd need more money—their money. These big wheels had just handed over many millions to buy a company they knew, and were rightly worried about making that work. Now I would ask them to spend even more on something they didn't understand, didn't even know existed. But I had planned ahead. I had witnesses.

Midway through my presentation to a crowd of about 100 executives, I stood on the stage and paused. It was plain they had heard enough description and needed only one answer: Whatever the hell this was, would it work? Would it make us money? Their skeptical looks and crossed arms told that story. They didn't fly halfway around the world to learn a new topic or get warm about one man's theories. Two alternatives must've raced through their businesslike minds: (1) keep, or (2) dump.

Scanning the crowd, I caught sight of Arthur, their

representative in Hong Kong. "Arthur," I asked, "how does this sound to you? Will this fly in the Pacific Basin?" Arthur rose and gave an affirmative reply. "I've looked it over and believe it will work in mainland China and Taiwan," he told the group, "and I've got some good ideas about Japan." Next I looked down at the woman who ran their Southern U.S. market. "Mary Ann, how do you see this applying in Atlanta, Miami, Dallas?" Mary Ann told them it would be a great fit with their insurance, finance, and manufacturing clients there. "We need something fresh," she concluded, "and this is a topic on every client's mind right now."

On I went to the man heading the business in South Africa. He stood and gave another positive reception. Then the French manager, and the Spanish one. But everyone knew, old-timers and new ones alike, that our firm had staked a good part of its future on the high-tech market—makers of computers, software, telecommunications. So I saved their ambassador for last. "James, is this the kind of thing we could use to spearhead a penetration of Silicon Valley, maybe lead us into consumer electronics as well?" James jumped to his feet and told of how they were struggling there. How they were just a face in the crowd of consultants slobbering over these growth industries. "We need something that distinguishes us from the rest," he concluded, "and this could be just the ticket. I want this. And if I can't have this, someone here has got to give me another hot service in its place." Somewhere in the back of my mind a film was playing. The scene was an old-time preacher pacing at the podium, embroiled in his message and rising to a fever pitch. "Can I get a witness?" he bellows. I got six of them.

And I was invited to the executive dinner at a posh London establishment that evening. I sat at the center table, and we—my newly enchanted owners and I— "were seen raising glasses in toast."

Witnesses vouch for the effort and validate the progress being made. Witnesses give testimony to the worth of your cause. They harmonize with your voice, backing up your enthusiasm. When you initiate the new among a group, seek out and find candidates for this role. Find the most influential and respected among them and work incessantly at converting them, and displaying them once converted. Witnesses are your living antidote to doubt and despair.

Witnesses provide the "surround sound" for your message.

That's also why it's so important to build milestones and other measures of intermediate success into any journey—physical witnesses, if you will. Some call these "early wins" and that's an apt name. We all need reassurance that we're making progress, closing the gap between where we are and where we want to be. Just like their literal counterparts, when passing these figurative indicators we receive positive reinforcement that, yes, we are going somewhere. We are making progress. This is going to work.

❏ The All-Stars of Compelling ❏

Let's look at the world's best. Here I'll use my own unscientific survey data. Across the earth I have used a technique to get audiences engaged in this discussion. I've taken a blank flipchart and asked them to list their choices for the most admirable people in history—people who have made an impact on all of us. I divide it into three categories, and record their nominations on the fly. From Helsinki to Beijing, from Buenos Aires to Toronto and on to Tokyo, Mexico City, Melbourne, and dozens of other places, the list started to take shape early and, with a few local exceptions, maintained a steadfast pattern. Across the globe, among many different cultures and heritages, the same people were cited as most compelling in each of these very different categories: (1) Politics and Society, (2) Art and Literature, and (3) Science and Technology. Table 4.2 is a compilation of the results.

The list may seem a bit Euro-centric, and maybe that's a function of where I've been, who attends, or just the pervasive influence of that heritage. Nonetheless, it gives us food for thought. Consider these insights:

Table 4.2   Compelling All-Stars

Politics and Society	Art and Literature	Science and Technology
Abraham Lincoln	Pablo Picasso	Thomas Edison
Winston Churchill	Cervantes	Galileo
Martin Luther King, Jr.	Dante Alighieri	Einstein
Mahatma Gandhi	Homer	Isaac Newton
Socrates	Voltaire	Louis Pasteur

1. Not one person on this list is remembered for keeping things exactly as they are. There are no stewards here. Each, in his own field, challenged and changed the way we all see, think about, and run our world—with huge implications and historic effect.

2. All suffered ridicule, and a surprising number were incarcerated for their thoughts and actions. Martin Luther King, Jr. was put in the Birmingham jail. Mahatma Ghandi was arrested and held behind bars. Galileo was castigated and imprisoned for heresy when contending the earth revolved around the sun. Einstein was humiliated after this unknown patent clerk had the audacity to publish his special theory of relativity. Pablo Picasso was seen as a crackpot, an amateur cartoonist, by the representational art establishment. Abraham Lincoln was called a moron and depicted in political cartoons as

an ape, a subhuman. Winston Churchill was driven from office. Dante was sentenced to death. Cervantes spent five years as an Algerian slave before penning Don Quixote. Voltaire was imprisoned in the Bastille for 11 months. After his death a group of "ultras" stole his remains and dumped them in a garbage heap. All of them went through Point B on the change curve.

3. Each can be evoked in our memory with a symbol or distinct image. Gandhi stooping over a salt marsh breaking the British prohibition against making salt, or spinning cloth on a hand loom. Dante's seven circles of hell. Lincoln standing at Gettysburg cemetery while a bloody war raged, reading his remarkably respectful address. Churchill's uplifting wartime radio assurances. Socrates' accepting poison rather than recanting his beliefs. A blind Homer reciting thousands of lines of poetry in his Iliad and Odyssey. Pasteur squinting into a microscope at the very causes of disease. Cervantes' Don Quixote tilting at windmills. And of course, Edison's light bulb is the very icon of a new idea.

4. Though Churchill's father was a renowned statesman, none of these men was born into royalty— there are no princes or kings here. Pasteur was the son of an impoverished tanner. Lincoln was born in a log cabin to a dirt-poor farmer. Galileo's father played the lute for a living and struggled to make

ends meet by teaching music. Newton's father was a farmer who couldn't sign his own name.

5. Each compelled a following, and achieved outcomes through others. These have lasted hundreds and even thousands of years and continue to affect us today. Each had a message: The world is different, or can be seen differently. And each lived that message—serving as his own first and best witness.

❏ I'm Not Making This Up ❏

I have never met Queen Elizabeth II or Nelson Mandela, but I've met esteemed leaders and some other unforgettable characters in high positions. One such person has a special place in my memory.

I was called by a recruiter asking me to interview for a major role in a blue-stocking consulting firm. The company had landed a huge contract extending years into the future and worth hundreds of millions of dollars, so they were staffing up. If they liked me, I'd receive an exceptional offer to be a "consultant to consultants" there for more than a year. Pay was good, the company was sound. I agreed to a two-stage interview. First I would meet a small group of principals for lunch in a private business club. Then, if I passed muster, I'd advance to a special meeting with the big boss—the man who would be my immediate supervisor should I be selected.

The lunch with the principals went well. Between courses I excused myself to visit the restroom. While I washed my hands at the sink, one of the principals entered and handed me his card, then quickly left—without using the facilities. "Turn it over," he said as he exited, heading back to the dining room. I did this, and read a handwritten note he'd jotted on the reverse of the card. "We really need leadership here," he wrote, "*please join us!*" His signature followed. So I agreed to continue to Stage Two, the interview with the senior vice president, who flew in to meet me a week later.

I arrived at their office on the top floor of a downtown bank building in my best business suit. The vice president met me at the elevator and reached a hand out. As I shook it, I saw a frayed sleeve extending from his suit jacket. Then he asked me to follow him to a private room. As we walked down the corridor, me trailing him, I couldn't help but notice his shoes. The heels were worn, excessively worn. Once seated behind closed doors, I listened to him go into a spiel about the company and what they expected from a successful candidate. They had high standards, he told me, they chose only the best. This extended right down to their dress code, he related proudly. For while other consulting firms allowed business-casual dress, this firm insisted on suits and ties at all times. "It's part of our professional image," he announced. "We want to look sharp when around clients."

All the while I was thinking of the down-at-the heels, frayed-shirt image seated in judgment of me. He kept on talking, and I pretended to listen. Then he turned his head just a fraction and I saw *it*. Extending from his right ear lobe was a hair that must've been at least three inches long! This thing was a monster, and when he nodded or shifted his head it waved around in the air like some sort of bullwhip. I tried to maintain a serious composure, but couldn't keep my eye off this undulating snake. I used all the restraint in my being, stifling a retch and a smile simultaneously. What was going on here? Was this some imposter taken off the street to trick me? Was this some surreal interview technique—some sort of test? Then it got even worse. As the interview concluded he lifted his massive body from his seat a few inches to shake my hand a final time and (I'm not making this up) abruptly, and quite audibly, passed gas. The man actually farted during my interview, and didn't miss a beat. Follow this guy into a new job? I didn't even follow him back to the elevator lobby.

This is a man who pulled down at least half a million dollars a year. He was undoubtedly well-educated and articulate, but Sgt. Johnson would've used a case of Kiwi on him. Riding down the elevator I pulled that restroom-delivered business card from my pocket and read it one more time. "We really need leadership here." Yes indeed. But what's this "We" stuff? Count me out.

There are hundreds of books, videos, seminars, and

the like that will help you prepare for and ace a job interview. But we're going to shift perspectives here again.
We move away from "standing in their shoes"—the perspective of the compelled (the interviewee) to the man
or woman on the other side of the table—the inter-
viewer, the leader. Most hiring managers forget that
their job is two-fold. They not only have to evaluate or
judge the candidate—they have to compel him or her to
join them. They're being interviewed as well. Are they
attracting the talent and enthusiasm of others, or pushing them away? Are they compelling, or like my ear-
whip acquaintance, *repelling* them? I've haunted the
book stores and done web searches on this, and advice
on how to conduct interviews, or more broadly, how to
compel others to join your cause, is rare. Becoming
compelling means looking, thinking, acting, and *being*
"like us and unlike us." It's not *tell* business, but *show*
business, as I've said before.

**No matter your cause, you are your first and best witness. Act
accordingly.**

Let's go further: It's not just show business, but *be* business. To compel, you must *be* what you espouse. You must
live what you cherish, act out your dream. Like the desper-
ate plea penned on the back of a business card handed me

by a disillusioned follower in the most unlikely of places, no matter whether we're trying to change a child's behavior, manage a corporation, or alter the way our government conducts itself, "We really need leadership here."

❏ There Are Zombies Among Us ❏

You'll find them on the freeway, driving right alongside you as you commute to work and back. They're riding silently on trains and buses, maybe even working undetected in the office cubicles all around you. They belong to your communities, wear your team uniforms, sit right next to you in theatres, and buy your company's goods and services; they're your neighbors. To the untrained eye and ear, they're indistinguishable from the rest of us. They seem to fit in, but some small thing—some hidden feature—is lacking, and only a few notice what it is.

You may have trouble detecting these subtle differences, but they're there nonetheless. If you look carefully, you'll notice them. They often exhibit a dull expression behind the eyes, a listless, going-through-the-motions attitude. They simply do what has to be done, sleepwalking through each day in dogged but low-keyed pursuit of what they need—not what they want. They want little or have given up wanting at all. They have no passion for what they're doing and little hope for making it better. Disillusioned, disgusted, disappointed, dejected. All apply.

People are sources of potential energy. Find it and ignite it.

Perhaps *zombies* is too harsh a term, but they are, in fact, asleep to their own potential. These are the people who desperately need leadership. They are fully capable of heroic, astonishing accomplishments if properly compelled—if given a message that challenges and inspires them, if placed in an environment that harnesses their expectations and matches their models of what they can do and what it means. If their cherished symbols are burnished anew or replaced with more honorable and appropriate emblems of who they are and how they fit into their worlds. If you can awaken their innate desire for improvement, if you can rekindle the smoldering embers inside most of them, you will affect outcomes.

They may seem listless and inert, even numb to anything more than the slightest incremental improvements, but they're more than this. Each is spring-loaded, waiting for the right touch, in the right way, for the right reasons. To be human is more than to use tools, language, or models—to be human is to aspire to quantum leaps in being and doing. To be prepared for the challenge and capable of the response. Both are waiting for you, and if you take this on, both are your responsibilities.

But first you must reexamine your intentions and your message. Are they inviting? Are they both logical and enchanting? Are you and your ideas respectful of the tangle of interwoven cultural pressures, the social thicket they inhabit? And most importantly, are you competent in the ways of magnetizing others to a larger cause, a higher Point C off in the future, and sustaining them through all the Point Bs they must traverse to attain it? Can you craft a dream and reshape your very self to deserve the privilege and honor of taking them there?

Are you trustworthy and genuine? Like Gandhi, who wrote "My life is my message," are you capable of serving as your own first and best symbol? Do you exude confidence, yet welcome the challenge of thinking and acting differently? Are you willing to abandon or postpone some of your own goals and preferences to achieve even greater, group ones? Have you invested your time and talent to learn how this is done, how to be even better at doing it? This is the price of making an impact through others, and that is not a trivial task nor to be taken lightly. Compelling others requires competence and courage. There can be no other way.

People may be enticed, even defrauded for a while, but they won't persist in counterfeit causes or tolerate manipulative falsehoods forever. Sooner or later, they'll look over their respective walls and notice a whole new way of being. Then they will drop whatever has deceived them to chase it, with their hearts and minds intact and engaged. You want them running toward, not away from you and your beliefs.

❑ I Did That ❑

I began this book with a short story involving my father, and I want to end it with one about his father, my grand-father. As a younger man he was a stonemason—a brick-layer—in a small town suffering through the Great Depression. Because our family traveled abroad for many years, I had never met him until a few weeks after my speaking debut in the mountains of Appalachia. My father drove my brothers and me to his decaying frame house for a brief visit. That afternoon, we piled into his ancient automobile and the old man took us on a tour of his home town.

First we passed the public library, one of the many depression-era, federally funded projects he worked on in those lean years. He reached a spotted, veined hand out the window and proudly proclaimed, "I did that!" Around a corner the town's high school came into view, red-bricked and still standing after decades of use. Again the hand, and again the comment: "I did that, too." Then past the waterworks, where stone was put upon stone by the man driving our car. Next came the post office, where he had toiled in the summer sun with bleeding knuckles so long ago, helping to create yet another enduring edifice. "I did that," he sighed, coughing up ancient brick dust and rock powder. As the town receded and we found his little cottage again, the old man turned to his progeny riding in the seat behind him and smiled—the way only one who has earned it can.

Few of us have the luxury of working on objects that stand for decades—on toiling at physical monuments we can later point to and say "I did that!" In our age, many of us work with intangibles, outcomes not so readily apparent. We sell insurance, teach children, settle lawsuits, write program code, manage youth leagues, research market trends, trade stocks, qualify mortgages, and the like. And yet we still have outcomes to achieve and others to affect.

When we get others to think and act differently, we are building the future no less than the man lifting stones and tamping mortar. We are responding to a challenge, creating what didn't exist before we arrived. If we are compelling, we enlist others in this. And one day, we may be taking our grandchildren past the indicators that we were, in fact, here. And we did, in fact, do that. Then they will know the answer to the perennial questions: *Who were you?* and *How did you fit into the world?*

Notes

Chapter 1: Message

1. Francis Bacon, *Novum Organum*, i, 41.

2. Will Durant, *Heroes of History* (New York: Simon & Schuster, 2001), 15.

3. Thomas Hobbes, *Leviathan*. "No arts; no letters; no society; and which is worst of all, continual fear and danger of violent death; and the life of man, solitary, poor, nasty, brutish, and short."

4. A provocative treatise on this is Julian Jaynes' *The Origin of Consciousness in the Breakdown of the Bicameral Mind* (Boston: Houghton Mifflin, 1976). Though hotly debated, it was internationally acclaimed and called "As startling . . . as Darwin's dissolution of species, as Einstein's reigning of light," by Richard Rhodes.

5. Arnold Toynbee, *A Study of History*. I particularly recommend the excellent two volume paperback abridgement by D. C. Sumervell for the Oxford University Press, 1946.

6. Erich Fromm, *Escape from Freedom* (New York: Henry Holt, 1941).

7. "A model is a provisional parallel taken from something outside the subject itself. It is useful when the nature of a thing is remote or obscure." Robert M. Augros and George N. Stanciu, *The New Story of Science* (Washington, DC: Regnery Publishing, 1984), 94.

Chapter 2: Reaction

1. Hugh Thomas, *Conquest: Montezuma, Cortes, and the Fall of Old Mexico* (New York: Touchstone, 1993).

2. Those interested in detailed explanations of phenomena like this should check out *Revolutionary Change*, by Chalmers Johnson (Palo Alto, CA: Stanford University Press, 1982).

Chapter 3: GroupThink

1. Erich Fromm, *The Sane Society* (New York: Ballantine Books, 1983), 41.

2. William Strauss and Neil Howe, *Generations: The History of America's Future, 1584 to 2069* (New York: William Morrow, 1991).

3. Ibid, 361.

4. A. Roger Ekrich, *At Day's Close* (New York: W.W. Norton, 2005).

5. Steven D. Levitt, and Stephen J. Dubner, *Freakonomics* (New York: HarperCollins, 2005), 25.

Notes

6. John Kenneth Galbraith, *The Culture of Contentment* (Boston: Houghton Mifflin, 1992), 69.

7. Henry David Thoreau, *Walden* (New York: New American Library, 1942), 9.

8. Kahlil Gibran, *A Tear and a Smile*, translated by H.M. Nahmad (New York: Alfred A. Knopf, 1950), 1.

Index

Index

Index

Index